W·H·I·T·E
BURGUNDY

CHRISTOPHER FIELDEN

Foreword by John Arlott

CHRISTOPHER HELM
London

THE WINE APPRECIATION GUILD
San Francisco

© 1988 Christopher Fielden
All photographs courtesy of Patrick Eagar
Christopher Helm (Publishers) Ltd, Imperial House,
21–25 North Street, Bromley, Kent BR1 1SD

ISBN 0–7470–1002–1

A CIP catalogue record for this book
is available from the British Library

Published in the United States by:
THE WINE APPRECIATION GUILD
155 Connecticut St.
San Francisco, CA 94107

ISBN 0–932664–62–8

Library of Congress No:

Typeset by Opus, Oxford
Printed and bound in Great Britain by
Billing and Sons Ltd, Worcester

Contents

To Robin

*May he take his pints
in Montrachet*

— if I can join him

Foreword

There was a call for this book, and Christopher Fielden was the man to write it. As he points out, there has been a long period — still not ended in many quarters — when the wine drinker's progress began with sweet white wine and then passed to dry white and on to the reds, Burgundy and then claret. Some, though, stayed all their lives with sweet white. Nowadays, however, many begin with dry white and continue with it for preference; it is the sophisticated white. No substantial work existed in English on the subject of dry white Burgundy: yet it is drunk here in increasing quantities.

There, then, lies the demand. Christopher Fielden had dealt in that demand for many years. He lived with his family for some four years in Burgundy, working for the major house of Chanson Père et Fils. He already had a good grounding in wine across the world, and French wine in particular, and began to travel his local Burgundy vineyards with immense interest. In point of fact, he is that rare character, the enthusiast whose enthusiasm survives work, commerce and study. For many years he has bought and sold wine with maximum interest: that interest has been reflected in intensive reading on the subject of wine in general, especially Burgundy wine, and on the history of the country of Burgundy. Enthusiasm makes what other people consider work, a pleasure. That is the keynote of Christopher Fielden's zest for his subject. Because of that drive and the extremely fluent French that he developed, he could talk to wine men there with ease: because of his interest he talked also with enthusiasm. It is apparent here when he lapses into French 'wine speak' that he has been able to talk in their 'in' language to those who make wine there: that is the key to this book, he understands the wine because he knows the men who make it. He is more than prepared to cede a point where he has not tasted a wine (and those instances are few) but he will fight his considered opinion against anyone.

From time to time he is illuminating, especially on such issues as 'plain Bourgogne'. He is no unnecessary romanticist; he can find the town of Chablis uninteresting, but he is absorbed by its wines. He is not necessarily pro-English nor pro-French but he obviously regrets his waning opportunities of 'sitting under the plane trees with a glass of Puligny in my hand watching a gentle game of cricket'.

For the ordinary interested traveller, Burgundy is a jumble of vineyards of red and white wines simply where they may be stumbled upon. Mr Fielden is understanding of our confusion when he writes of Musigny, one of only two grands crus in Burgundy producing both red and white wine. Talking of its output of just over four hogsheads of white, he observes 'Its resemblance to a traditional white Burgundy is minimal and there are some who claim that when tasted blind it is often mistaken for red wine. At the price that is asked for it I feel that it is a pity to drink it blind. You need all your wits about you.'

He is concerned, too, with the buyer of wine — 'Increasing demand from around the world has meant that the consumer has had to pay more for the great wines of Burgundy. Many of us are having to look elsewhere for the taste of Chardonnay. It is not always necessary to look outside Burgundy. While the novelty wines of the Côte de Nuits are expensive, there are still bargains to be had with such wines as Saint-Aubin and Auxey-Duresses, not to mention the wines of the Haute-Cotes.' (He used to live there and retains a local palate.)

This is an expert book written with a friendly — even humorous — touch by a man who wishes to share his pleasure in all wine and, in this instance, particularly in Burgundy. There is an urge constantly to quote him with an air of 'listen to this'. 'Whilst the inhabitants of France might be drinking less wine overall, they are drinking more good wine. Around the world it is at the bottom end of the market that there is a rapid decline. It is not the wine of the wine lakes that people are seeking. They realize that, by paying a little more, good, and even great wines, are to be had.'

Here Mr Fielden provides valuable guidance in an outstanding bibliography, and his tables — concise and adequate without being elaborate — of the white wine appellations of Burgundy, and recommended producers. This book though, is perhaps most valuable for its recording of Mr Fielden's outstanding wine asset — his palate — which he is prepared to defend in virtually any field, and with immense gusto.

John Arlott

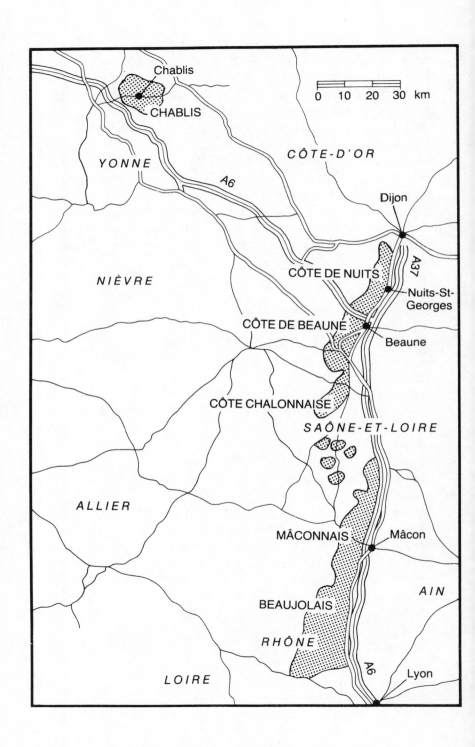

1
Introduction

The past few years have seen a radical change in the consumption of wine. Just this morning I have received a list of the top ten countries in the league of per capita wine consumption. France and Italy, which have led the table in the past, have now been overtaken by Portugal, which is the only country in the table to show a significant increase. However, whilst the inhabitants of France might be drinking less wine overall, they are drinking more good wine. Around the world it is at the bottom end of the market that there is a rapid decline.

As affluence spreads throughout the developed world, the consumer seeks to improve his status, and what he eats and drinks has always proved to play an important role in this improvement. In addition to the radical change in drinking habits of the traditional wine-consuming countries, there are also opening up vast new markets in those countries which have not been recognised as major wine-drinkers. In the United States, Great Britain, Australia and Canada alone there are potentially enough willing drinkers to solve any problem that the largest of wine lakes might present. However, once again, it is not the wines of the wine lakes that such people are seeking. They realise that, by paying a little more, good and even great wines are to be had.

It is the new affluent, many of whom are comparatively young, who are the seekers after truth in the world of wine. One has only to listen to a group of American wine buffs talking together to discover how seriously fine wine is now taken by many people. Often I feel that much of the pleasure

1

disappears from the drinking of wine if you have to talk about it for too long either beforehand or afterwards. However it is just this sort of person who is coming to the wines of Burgundy, and more particularly to the white wines.

When the dollar was at its strongest in the early 1980s — and the franc was at its weakest — the American public's thirst, for even the finest and most expensive white wines of Burgundy, seemed almost unassuageable. Now white wine has replaced the martini as the fashionable aperitif, and the sad situation whereby it was often impossible to obtain a glass of wine with your meal in the United States is now, happily, a thing of the past.

This rapid expansion in the demand for white wine seems to have taken the wine-growers of the world by surprise. The drinker is scarcely interested in the fact that wine is not an instant product, that red and white wines do not come out of the tap, like at one hotel in Dijon. For many traditional vineyard areas, which over the centuries have made their living by producing red wines, the situation has been dramatic. In areas of perhaps greater flexibility, like California and Australia, white vines can be grafted on to red rootstock, or 'blush' wines can try to disguise as white wines those made from grapes normally destined for the red wine vat. For the purist, the concept of a white Zinfandel must come as an unwelcome surprise.

Burgundy's world of wine is innately conservative. Its vineyards lack the flexibility of the New World. Red wine has been made on this plot of land for 1,000 years or more; it is impossible to change. Habitudes, the soil and legislation dictate it. That Californian growers like Bill Jekel have demonstrated that the same soil can produce great wines from a broad variety of grapes, in a broad variety of styles, is irrelevant. Over the years Burgundy has built up its reputation mainly with its red wines; first response to increasing demand for its white wines has been to increase prices.

However, such a policy can have very dangerous results. As I write this, the dollar is under pressure and the demand for the great wines of France from the United States has dropped dramatically. The collapse of price in some white

Burgundies has been nothing less than dramatic, with the wines of Pouilly-Fuissé now selling for less than a third of their price a year and a half ago.

While an expansion in the area of vines in Burgundy is strictly controlled, there are possibilities in certain areas, for vineyards may be planted where there have been vineyards in the past. Both the phylloxera plague, at the end of the eighteenth century, and the First World War led to the abandonment of vineyard cultivation in parts of Burgundy. This is particularly true of Chablis, the Côte Chalonnaise and the Hautes-Côtes de Beaune and Nuits. In addition, especially in the Mâconnais, many vineyards that until recently used to make cheap red wines from the Gamay, have now been replanted with the Chardonnay to make white wines. As you will see, particularly in Chablis, there has been criticism about some of the new vineyards, saying in the main that their soil is not ideal for the production of fine wines.

It must also be borne in mind that improved methods of viticulture and vinification are leading not only to the production of better wines, but also to higher yields. Whilst, for the grower, there might have been financial advantages in restricting the size of the crop to maintain high prices, now greater demand has meant that this is a short-sighted policy. It is generally accepted now that, particularly for white wines, the restricted yields of the past were totally unrealistic and had no appreciable beneficial effect on the quality of the wine. The enormous crop of 1973 came as an eye-opener to the growers and that paled into insignificance when the final statistics were worked out for the yield of the 1982 vintage. The authorities, and they are generally controlled by the growers, have now accepted the realities of life and the maximum yield per hectare now varies from vintage to vintage. Permitted crops are now, in most years, considerably higher than they were under the old legislation.

The rapid increase in the availability of white Burgundies is illustrated by the following statistics from different editions of that most valuable source book on the wines of Burgundy, *Les Vins de Bourgogne*, by Pierre Poupon and Pierre Forgeot.

Hectolitres — average production per annum

	1952	1959	1964	1983	1985
Bourgogne Aligoté	36,000	35,500	45,400	36,000	45,500
Mâcon Villages/	45,000	52,650	76,900	86,500	103,200
Supérieur (white)					
Pouilly-Fuissé	16,000	16,000	19,700	32,000	36,100
Montagny	1,600	1,622	2,105	2,800	3,800
Chablis Grand Cru	620	478	545	4,500	5,300
Chablis/Chablis ler Cru	8,500	7,650	9,900	60,000	89,150
Meursault (white)	7,566	7,566	8,750	15,100	14,700
le Montrachet	100	110	133	220	316
and for comparative purposes,					
the red wine Volnay	4,800	4,900	5,400	7,200	7,300

By studying these figures, much can be learnt about the development of the white wines of Burgundy. It is interesting to note that, with the one exception of Bourgogne Aligoté, which is produced from the Aligoté grape and over the period in question has been largely grubbed up and replaced with Chardonnay, in all appellations there has been a considerable increase in production. It is not difficult to understand the increase of almost 1,000 per cent in the figures for Chablis, for the area under vines has been considerably extended and protection against frost has now largely been perfected. On the other hand, the vineyard area for Montrachet has remained constant, yet there has been an increase in the average annual yield of more than 200 per cent. The Chablis Grand Cru vineyard area has not increased either, but the production has by more than 750 percent. It is true that in former times, the Chablis vineyards lay fallow for long periods, but even so, this is a truly remarkable increase.

An idea of what improved husbandry alone can do is probably best given by the figures for Volnay and Meursault, where the increases in the crop have been less noteworthy. Certainly there has been some recuperation of vineyards from scrubland in Meursault, but in Volnay the area under vines will scarcely have changed during the years under review.

There the increase is some 52 per cent, and this is typical of the red wine production. The relative importance of white wines in the total Burgundy picture has therefore increased at an exceptionally fast rate. If one considers the total *appellation contrôlée* wine production of the four *départements* of Burgundy, the Yonne, the Côte d'Or, Saône et Loire and the Rhône, white wine accounts for less than 20 per cent of the total, but if one excludes the Rhône, with its sea of Beaujolais, which is almost entirely red, the white wine proportion is nearer 40 per cent.

In overall production terms, Burgundy is not a major vineyard area, for in an average year more than two and a half times as much wine comes out of Bordeaux. Nevertheless on export markets white Burgundy is the wine that has been in demand. In terms of value it represented 37 per cent of the total exports of white *appellation contrôlée* French wines during the commercial year of 1985/86. In terms of volume it was a substantial 16 per cent. (The comparable figures for red Burgundies are 15 and 8 per cent respectively.) During the same period over 40 per cent of the exports of white Burgundy went for the American market. It is also interesting to note that the exports in terms of hectolitres fell overall by no less than 16 per cent, as opposed to the previous year, with the leading seven foreign markets, which account for more than nine-tenths of sales, all having registered falls.

The taste of the Chardonnay grape appears to be the taste of the future. Today's wine-drinker prefers year by year the dry taste of the wines of Burgundy to the sweeter flavours of Germany. This pressure is having its effect on prices. Whilst the better wines of Burgundy have never been cheap, they were not expensive, as long as they remained the preferred wine of the connoisseur and not a wine for the general consumer.

It is interesting that in Victorian times, when a true appreciation of individual wines in England became much more widespread, the writers devoted comparatively little space to the white wines of Burgundy, apart from Montrachet, which was lauded as one of the great wines of the world and invariably mentioned in the same breath as the other great white wine delights of the time, which were, for the most part, sweet. James Denman, in 1845, describes Montrachet as, 'the champion wine of the province, at once its Château Yquem, Johannisberger, and Imperial Tokay, which every native Burgundian pronounces to be the grandest white wine on the face of the globe'. Other white Burgundies are granted in totality half as much space as the eulogy on Montrachet.

Ninety years later, Stephen Gwynn, in his book on the wines of Burgundy, devotes a chapter to the wines of Chablis, approximately two pages on the white wines of the Côte d'Or and nothing to the wines of the Mâconnais, apart from a brief mention of Pouilly-Fuissé.

There are, therefore, two good reasons for giving the white wines of Burgundy their individual recognition, separate from that of the red wines. First of all, they have for long been recognised as great wines, though at certain times comparatively unknown. Secondly, and perhaps more relevantly, they are now representative of the style of wine that seems to appeal to the ever widening field of wine-lovers around the world. It used to be said that the four stages in the life of the wine-lover were; sweet white wines, dry white wines, red Burgundy and claret. Many drinkers never advanced beyond the first step on this ladder. Now many are starting, and even staying, on the second step. White Burgundy has a major role as the solid centre of this second step.

The wine region of Burgundy is not the same as the French administrative province of the same name, but its reputation is more widely spread. Its vineyards form just a minor part of the four *départements* of the Yonne, the Côte d'Or, Saône et Loire and the Rhône. They are but one part of the largely agricultural whole. This is one of the strengths of the region. Few wines are great on their own; they demand good food to accompany them. The two classic partners for white wine are fish and chicken. Burgundy is watered by a succession of rivers, the Saône, the Doubs, the Yonne, the Serein, the Dheune and the Ouche. From them come the fish for that most Burgundian of fish dishes, the *pochouse*, a blend of carp, tench, perch, eel and pike cooked in white wine and marc de Bourgogne. This is the speciality of the riverside restaurants, so popular on summer weekends, at Seurre and Verdun sur le Doubs, the spiritual home of the *pochouse*, or *pauchouse*, as it is sometimes spelt.

From the smaller streams, if you are lucky, there are crayfish to be caught in the summer. More common are the classic snails of Burgundy, though whether they should be accompanied by a red wine or a white, is a matter of some debate. The collecting of snails is taken very seriously in Burgundy, and it is not uncommon to see, rather like the ubiquitous *chasse réservée* sign, one saying *ramassage d'escargots défendu*. As in any form of serious hunting, there is a close season; from 15 May to 10 September. There is no one more dedicated to the defence of the snail than the Burgundian writer Henri Vincenot. He is a pillar of the brotherhood dedicated to the protection of the interests of the snail, which each year gives an award to the individual who has made an outstanding effort on behalf of *helix pomathia*. If one is to believe Monsieur Vincenot, the snail has played an important part in the development of Burgundy. When the main railway line was built from Paris to the Mediterranean, the surveyors were worried that where the line crossed the hills that separated the rivers flowing into the English Channel from those that flowed southwards to the Mediterranean, there were so many snails that the carnage on the rails would prevent the engines getting the necessary grip for the steep inclines. As a result the railway line does not go over the hills, but rather through them, by the tunnel of Blaisy.

What is so special about chicken in Burgundy? For someone brought up on the fish-meal-fed, factory-farmed chicken that we find so frequently in Britain, it is a relevation. The tasty, yellowish flesh, which comes from running free and a diet of maize, is a gastronomic world away. Across the river Saône from Mâcon lies the Bresse. Nowhere in France, or in the world for that matter, has a higher reputation for its poultry. The local producers are so jealous of their reputation that they have created for themselves an *appellation contrôlée* whose regulations are as severe as those for any wine.

Even though white wines in Burgundy are taking a more important role, there are comparatively few areas where red and white wines are produced side by side. The soil, or perhaps more importantly the subsoil, is the controlling factor. As a rule of thumb, chalky soil is better for white wines and where this is evident, white wine is made. Thus, the major areas of production for white wine are the Chablis region in the Yonne, the southern part of the Côte de Beaune, on the Côte d'Or (which is occasionally called the Côte de Meursault); part of the Côte Chalonnaise and the Mâconnais, from the Saône et Loire. Little white wine is made elsewhere and on the Côte de Nuits and in the Beaujolais, the proportion is minuscule.

Whether the current vogue for the white wines of Burgundy will last is not for me to say. As they are at the present, they offer a fascinating mosaic and I hope that this book will give a glimpse at least of the pieces that go to make up that mosaic.

2
White Burgundy in History

For two reasons it is not easy to write a history of the white wines of Burgundy. First, there is really only one story to tell about the wines of Burgundy; red, white and a little bit of rosé are all intermixed threads that are woven together to make one tapestry; separately they mean very little. The second reason is perhaps even more basic. In early writings, wines were little described. Vineyards were mentioned frequently from the earliest times, but not much was said about what they produced. Burgundy was a name for a wine from a region and it appears that the fact that it was white or red, or, as was often the case, somewhere between the two, was rarely mentioned.

When the Romans arrived in Gaul, the area that is now largely Burgundy was inhabited by a Celtic tribe, the Aedui. According to the local historian Gandelot their 'Republic stretched in the East as far as the Saône; in the West to the Loire and the Allier; to the streams of the Roins and the Ardière in the South; the regions of Langres and Auxois in the North . . . Also under its authority were the people of the Forez, the Beaujolais and part of the Lyonnais.' Pliny says that the tribe already drank wine and it is probable that this came to them in the form of trading, for they controlled a vital segment of one of the most important prehistoric trade routes, the Tin Road, from Cornwall to the Western Mediterranean.

Pierre Forgeot even suggests that they might have made wine themselves, having learnt the art from the time that they settled in Northern Italy between the fifth and second centuries BC. There are traces of wine consumption in Burgundy from well before the arrival of the Romans, but the earliest proof of vineyards dates from Roman times. It was in Burgundy that the final overthrow of the Gauls by Julius Caesar took place and his memory remains in the name of a grape, the César, that is still used for the production of red wine in the Yonne *département*.

Lyons became the capital of Roman Gaul and an important staging post on the military route to that frontier of the Empire, where the Romans were to fight for centuries, the Rhine. Burgundy lay well behind the front line and was a totally peaceful province, with the military encouraged to spend time in agricultural and viticultural pursuits. Many of the villages whose names are now given to the greatest wines of the Côte d'Or, such as Aloxe-Corton and Volnay, probably began their existence as Roman villas, surrounded by the houses of their dependants; Beaune lay close to where the two major Roman roads of the province crossed, the Agrippan Way, which led from Lyons to the frontier on the Rhine and the other from Autun, the new capital of the Aedui, named in honour of the Emperor, Augustodunum, to Vesontio (Besançon). In the third century a Roman camp was established in the town; one that was important enough to have at lest two temples; one dedicated to the Celtic God of springs, Belenus, who became absorbed in the worship of Apollo, and the other, perhaps with foresight, to Bacchus.

The region was known for the excellence of its horses and the troops throughout Gaul were supplied from the neighbourhood. Where and at what point was wine made by the Romans here? This is a difficult question to answer. At the end of the first century AD, the Emperor Domitian decreed that all vineyards outside Italy should be grubbed up, first to increase the supply of corn for an ever-expanding empire and secondly to protect the home industry. Whilst this edict was not repealed until 281 AD, by the Emperor Probus, it is generally considered that it was of little relevance in

Burgundy. It is almost certain that wine was produced by many of the local landowners, if only for 'family' consumption. Indeed a stela dating from the middle of the second century, found near Corgoloin, depicts a vineyard worker with a vine-shoot in one hand and a pruning-knife in the other.

The first document which talks in detail of the vineyards of Burgundy is a report made by Eumenius, a representative of Burgundian viticultural interests to the Emperor Constantine, in Autun in 312 AD. He speaks of the reputation that the vineyards have, but claims that it is unmerited because of the poorness of the soil and the intemperate climate. 'These vines, admired so greatly by those who cannot see the real condition that they are in, are so worn out with age that it is doubtful if they benefit from the care that we lavish upon them. Their roots, whose age we cannot know, with their thousand twistings have formed such a mass that we cannot dig the ditches as deep as we would like, so that their shoots, for want of sufficient cover, are exposed to the rains that drown them and the sun which burns them.' One can almost imagine the writer putting in a similar plea for special consideration to the Common Market authorities in Brussels today!

The fourth century saw the arrival of Christianity in Burgundy as the dominant religion, a situation that was achieved at the price of several martyrs. The success of Christianity was the fact that was to carry forward the wines of Burgundy during the dark period after the sack of Rome and collapse of its empire during the fifth century. It was during the previous century that the three great bishoprics of Burgundy were established, those of Auxerre, Autun and Langres. (It is interesting that those of Autun and Langres were based on the former capitals of the two great Celtic tribes of history, the Aedui and the Lingones.)

That viticulture did continue after the departure of the Romans is apparent from the writings of the sixth century ecclesiastical historian, Gregory of Tours. He noted that the Bishop of Langres spent more time in the town of Dijon, to be near his vineyard holdings, then he did in Langres itself and that 'there was no member of the aristocracy who did not wish to have in his cellars some of the wine of Burgundy'. Some idea of the rating of local wines can also be gained by his description of the neighbourhood of Dijon. 'To the West the hills are covered with fruitful vines, which yield so noble a Falernian-style wine that the inhabitants have been known to scorn a good Mâcon.'

The role of the church in the production, distribution and reputation of the wines of Burgundy was primordial from the departure of the Romans until the French Revolution at the end of the eighteenth century. From the earliest times, they became the most important vineyard owners. In 650 AD, Amalgaire leaves his vineyards in Larrey and Couchey to the Abbey of Beze at Vosne; in 775 the Emperor Charlemagne gives his vineyards in Pernand and Aloxe to the Abbey at Saulieu and the Bishop of Autun in 858 passes on his vines in Aloxe to the Cathedral chapter.

The importance of vineyards in the Burgundian way of life is recognised by one of the greatest penal codes of the time, the Lex Gombetta, drawn up by the Burgundian King Gondebaud, at Ambérieu in 506. Whilst 100 lashes was the penalty for a slave striking a free man, anyone has the right to plant a vineyard in an uncultivated field.

Charlemagne, too, drew up a code of practice, in 70 paragraphs, for his agricultural managers, with detailed instructions being given, as to the cleanliness of wine material, that only top quality casks should be used for the better ageing of the wine and that the grapes should not be pressed by foot.

As well as having three major sees, Burgundy was also an important missionary centre. Even Saint Patrick spent part of his life studying in Auxerre. The guiding feature, however, of this spread of the gospel was the monastic orders, and Burgundy was at the centre of what were probably the two most important orders of medieval times, the Benedictines and the Cistercians.

In 909 AD Duke William of Aquitaine gave a chapel and a small farm in the valley of the Grosne, a tributary of the Saône, for the establishment of a monastic house. The Duke, however, wished this to be rather different from other orders, for he travelled to Rome to entrust it personally to the authority of the Pope. Herein lay the real strength of the monastery at Cluny: it was answerable to no local ecclesiastic — and decisions might be long in coming from Rome. Very rapidly its power spread and it was to become the most important landowner in Burgundy. Amongst this land were many vineyards, mostly in what is now known as the Mâconnais, though there were also holdings on the Côte d'Or, including much of Gevrey.

The monastic life at Cluny varied considerably from that which had been prescribed by Saint Benedict. The seven hours manual work per day were forgotten and the estates were looked after by paid hands. Instead, Cluny became an intellectual and artistic hothouse, a haven for the finest architects and illuminators of the day. The library was full of works both sacred and profane and some of these latter so shocked a number of the Abbots that they sought to restrict others from reading them.

Some monks began to feel that the monastic life at Cluny was not at all what they had expected when they took their vows and three of them, including the Englishman Stephen Harding, left in 1098 to establish a more ascetic order at Citeaux to the east of Nuits. Here, in what were inhospitable marshy surroundings, began what was to become the Cistercian order. Sadly, perhaps, within a matter of years, this order began to attract the bequests of the wealthy nobility and it also rapidly built up important wine estates centred on its press-house and cellars in the village of Gilly-lès-Vougeot. Under the patronage of Eudes I, Duke of Burgundy and his liege lord, Reynald, Viscount of Beaune, the Cistercians rapidly increased in monastic importance, whilst that of the Benedictines went into slow decline.

The importance of these monastic orders in medieval life cannot be underestimated. The Abbot of Cluny's direct access to the Pope, as well as the fact that he was, at the peak of his powers, responsible for 1,400 subsidiary monastic houses, whose Abbots were all appointed by him, meant that his wines were drunk widely throughout the civilised world.

The last of the great Abbots, Peter the Venerable, was personally involved in the organisation of the disastrous second crusade and this also helped to spread the renown of his wines.

Whilst the Cistercians might upbraid the Cluniacs by accusing them of taking 'so much pleasure in the lies of the poets, that you read, study and teach them even in the hours which Saint Benedict has definitely reserved for the reading of Scriptures and for manual labour', they too were introducing their wines though the twin networks of the nobility and the church.

The extension of the Cistercian order led to the building of yet another major monastery in the world of the wines of Burgundy. In 1114, the Abbey of Pontigny was built on the banks of the River Serein in what is now the Chablis region. The monks leased some vines four years later from the Benedictines of Saint Martin de Tours, who had been originally granted land in the area by Charles the Bald, as a haven against Viking attacks. The connections between Pontigny and Britain were particularly strong as it served as a retreat for no less than three Archbishops of Canterbury, Thomas à Becket, Stephen Langton and St Edmund of Abingdon, an important ecclesiastical politician of the thirteenth century.

Indeed one of the earliest mentions of a white wine of Burgundy is indirectly connected with Thomas à Becket. In 1178, William of Champagne, Archbishop of Reims, was returning from a pilgrimage to the saint's shrine and was being entertained by the Count of Guignes, at Ardres, just south of Calais. The hospitality was generous and a number of the guests began to complain about the strength of the Greek wine that was being served to them and asked for some jugs of water to weaken it. Jugs were brought, but the wine continued to take its toll and it appears that the Count, rather than offer water, had asked his servants to bring jugs of the crystal-clear white wine of Auxerre.

This period seems to have been the beginning of the great reputation of the white wines of the region, which could be easily distributed to Paris and the north down the River

Yonne and its tributaries on flat-bottomed barges. It is known that much red wine was also made, but the fact that just three years later Anseric II, High Steward of Burgundy, and his wife Sybille, gave their vineyards in Chablis to the monks of Pontigny, assuring them that it gave a good white wine 'that one can keep for a long time', leads one to think that white wines were more fashionable.

In 1203, John Lackland, as the French call him, or King John as he is known to the English, celebrated the resolution of a dispute between the Count of Leicester and the Bishop of Lincoln by broaching a cask or two of wine from Auxerre, which experts considered to be the best of all wines as it was 'as white as spring water'.

In 1215, the monks of Saint Martin de Tours sought to extend their vineyard holdings in the neighbourhood of Chablis, and as they did not have enough ready money in their coffers to pay the 2,000 *livres* that the owner, Guy de Montéral, asked for his vineyard, they did not hesitate to melt down and sell off some of the gold plate that covered the High Altar in the Abbey. This says much for their sense of priorities. Presumably land was a better investment than gold.

At this time Bourgogne was a generic name for the wines that came from what is now the Yonne *département*. Those wines that came from further south were called either Beaune or Mâcon. A comparative rating of the standing of the wines can be judged from the entry tolls that wines had to pay into Paris in 1337. It may be though that there was some regional preference for those wines that were more readily available:

France (Ile de France)	1⅓ sous
Bourgogne (Auxerre)	2 sous
Gascogne (Bordeaux)	4 sous
Beaune	5 sous

There can be little doubt that the wines of Auxerre were fashionable, for in 1342 Pope Clement VI appointed his own wine-buyer based in the region. It also seems that it was the white wines that were still in vogue for an inventory taken of the Duke of Burgundy's cellar in Lille in 1388, shows that nine-tenths of the stock was white wine. Nevertheless when the envoys of the King of England were being entertained in Bruges thirteen years before, the quality drinking was done with red Burgundy; the white was just used for slaking thirst.

At this time the Duchy of Burgundy was an important territory which, since the marriage of Philippe le Hardi to Marguerite of Flanders in 1369, included much of what we know now as Holland and Belgium. The titles of Charles le Téméraire, a century later, give a clear idea of the standing that the Dukes had in the affairs of Europe. He was 'Duke of Burgundy, of Lothier (Basse-Lorraine), of Luxembourg, of Limbourg, and of Gueldres, Count of Artois, of Flanders and of Burgundy, Palatine of Hainault, of Holland, of Zeeland, of Namur and of Zutphen, Marquis of the Holy Empire, Lord of Friesia, of Salins and of Malines' and there were still many more to come.

This importance of Burgundy in the temporal world as well as the ecclesiastical meant even more that its wines came to be appreciated widely, with the wines of Auxerre being sent mainly towards the north and those of Beaune being dispatched to the south and east. Whilst we have traces of growers in what are now the great white wine villages of the Côte d'Or from this time (Jean de Chassaignes had vines in Montrachet in 1308), we have no real record of the specific white wines of the period. In any case the vogue for white wine must have been overtaken by harsh reality. Red wine is easier to keep than white wine and it travels much better. As a result, it is probable that by the end of the fourteenth century the increase in the production of red wine, at the expense of white, was well under way. Raymond Dumay in *Le Vin de Bourgogne* would like to place the key date in this move towards red wine as the Bruges banquet in 1375. Then, he suggests, the superiority of the red wine was recognised, by keeping back the comparatively small quantities made available for the important guests.

What is clear is that, at that time and for many centuries to come, it was the exception if white grapes and red were grown separately, or even vinified separately. It was felt until the end of the eighteenth century that all red wines benefited from having a proportion of white grapes in their composition. As Abbé Bavard says in his work on the wines of Volnay, which was published in Dijon in 1870, 'Formerly on the slopes of Volnay and the other great villages of Burgundy, the Pinot Noir was mixed with the Pinot Blanc; the proportion of the latter often rose to an eighth of the total number of vines. This was how it was until the beginning of the last century. Since then, these plants have been grubbed up. Some notable oenologists regret the disappearance of this factor; for, they say, the grapes of this variety, crushed and put in small quantities in the vat, take from the wine none of its colour, but on the contrary give it class, delicacy, life and make it last longer.' The vineyards, too, were not the neatly organised fields that one sees today. As a result of the regeneration of the vines by *provignage*, or burying of the young shoots to regenerate the new plants, the vines grew much more closely together and without any sort of order.

For the most part yields were much lower than they are today and this has been given as one reason why the wines of those times must have been of superior quality. Sadly this argument if carried to its logical extreme, would stand in the way of many of the advances that have taken place in agriculture and in viticulture.

What grape varieties were grown in these times? Here again it must be realised that ampelography, the study of individual varieties, did not really develop until the nineteenth century, and whilst a substantial number of different grapes were recognised, there was much confusion as to what was really what and there must have been considerable intermingling of varieties. Puvis, writing as late as the middle of the nineteenth century says that most Burgundian growers of the previous century felt that the merits of any particular grape variety came from the region where it grew rather than from the grape itself. Nevertheless it is apparent from the continual efforts that were made to ban the Gamay from the vineyards of the Côte d'Or, that most people knew that certain grapes made better wine in smaller quantities and that others were capable of producing much larger quantities of inferior wine.

The anonymous author of *Les Délices de la Campagne*, which first appeared in 1654, was a particular fan of the wines of Chablis and he says of the making of white wines in general, 'The best white grape plants for making dry wine are the Meslier, the Beaune and the Fromentier.' This last grape appeared under a number of names, but was probably best known as the Fromenteau. The general feeling is that it took its name from the flour made from *froment* or wheat, which was the finest and whitest throughout the middle ages. Pierre Forgeot, on the other hand, would like to believe that it comes from the name of a village that lay on the Tin Road bearing the same name. As he says, the Burgundy villages of Gamay, Chasselas and Chardonnay all gave their names to grapes, so why not Fromenteau? This grape was most probably the Pinot Gris, which is still called the Fromentot in Champagne, but is now the Pinot Beurot in Burgundy. The main black grape in Burgundy was the Morillon, the Pinot, which was also grown as a white variety. Amongst the other white grapes grown in Burgundy, according to an eighteenth-century writer, were the Bourguignon Blanc (sometimes known as the Mourlon or Clozier), the Bourdelais (called the Gray in Burgundy) and the Beaunier (named the Servinien in Auxerre).

The time of the vintage was controlled by the municipal authorities as described by a contemporary. 'A month before the vintage, the magistrates of Beaune, accompanied by many experienced judges and persons of probity, make three visits to examine the maturity of the grapes; and at this third visit and examination, they decide the day of gathering the vintage. No private person dares to cut in his own vineyard one single basket of grapes upon pain of confiscation and a considerable fine; for if it were permitted to each particular person to gather his vintage according to his own fancy, his particular opinion, and according to his taste, there would be wines too green sent abroad into other countries, to the dishonour of Burgundy and to the discredit of the wines.'

This system of *ban de vendanges* was not widely popular, as is apparent from a petition on the subject made to the Prefect of the Côte d'Or shortly after the French Revolution.

In it the *ban* is described as 'the favoured child of feudal times' as it gave the nobility a head's start by allowing them to pick their grapes a day before anyone else, and thus find their customers more quickly.

In *Les Délices de la Campagne*, the author also gives details as to how to make a dry white wine. 'Gather the white grapes after the red ones have been harvested, crush them in a vat which is used just for white wines and wash the press well, before pressing the *marc*, to avoid taking on any red traces; then throw everything in the vat and let it ferment until it has lost all trace of sweetness and taste of the must.' Surprisingly, the author suggests that this wine is useful for giving vigour to red wines and for making them more highly appreciated by innkeepers, who apparently were in the habit of offering a *Cuvée à Deux*, or mixture of light red and white wine. He also mentions a German habit of burning sulphur tapers in casks before filling them.

Quite what the wines tasted like during this period is not at all clear. The Nuits Saint Georges house of Geisweiler offers its customers a range of Burgundies in what it calls the styles of the fifteenth, eighteenth and nineteenth centuries. Whilst they have been able to establish distinctive characters in the red wines, these are much less well defined as far as the white wines are concerned. Abbe Tainturier, writing in 1763, gives as the prime quality of a white Burgundy, that it should be 'dry'. Given the fact that sweet wines were quite widely made at the time, this requirement is less self-evident than it might appear. Indeed when one reads of Arnoux' description of the white wines of Meursault as being 'delicious, sparkling, agreeable, warm and beneficial', one wonders quite what sort of wines were made.

The interest in white wines received a powerful stimulus as a result of developments during the eighteenth century. The first was the increasing use of bottles for the ageing and shipment of wine after their production began on a commercial scale in 1750. Until that time most shipping had been done in cask and the white wines, particularly, were likely to suffer from oxidation. That bottles were used before this date is apparent from what Arnoux has to say on the problem:

It remains for me to relate how these wines may be brought to England. It has always been the custom to bring those wines from Burgundy in their casks; but as the carriage is long, and there is oftentimes a risque run, so the carriers, as well by land as by sea, are not always faithful; for notwithstanding all the precaution that can be taken to hinder them from drinking the wine, they will always find out stratagems to do it. If it be packed up in casks with straw and linen cloths, this is but a feeble obstacle to their industry. As for all this precaution, if the cask happens to leak on the way this will be at the peril and loss of the purchaser. If these wines be put into double casks, this precaution will have no better success than the foregoing, and is exposed to the same risque; and the casks at the vintages are a great prejudice to these delicate wines, because this gives the full scope to the spirits to evaporate: and of consequence this will cause a great diminution of the quality of the wine.

It ought to be brought in bottles from Beaune to London . . . The agent might bottle up these wines a year after the vintage, either more or less; and the purchasers might receive the wines of Burgundy exquisite and delicious.

The other great happening of the time was the progression of the status of the 'agent' that Arnoux has just mentioned. Until the end of the seventeenth century, the control of the quality of wine and much of the selling was in the hands of the municipally appointed officials, the *courtiers gourmets*, of whom there are traces in Beaune, as early as the fourteenth century, when we even know the names of two of them, Guillaume Lorette and Odet Berbizotte. Each year, they officially tasted the new wine and a price was established by a committee consisting of all the interested parties. No wine was allowed to leave the town until after this meeting, and until it had been sealed by the *courtier*.

At the end of the seventeenth century, it appeared that the *courtiers* became more lax in the application of the law and there grew up a new group, called *commissionaires*, who would buy wine on their own account and on that of their customers in France and abroad. Such men would be the 'agents' of whom Arnoux talks, as was probably also Bazin, the cooper from the northern suburbs of Beaune, who bought wine for Thomas Jefferson.

Towards the middle of the eighteenth century, the merchants that we know today began to establish themselves and they actively sought out customers throughout Western Europe. The first merchant, in 1720, was Edmé Champy, and he was followed in the next thirty years by Joseph Amyot, Michel Bouchard, Jean-Gerard Labaume, Philibert Poulet and Simon Very. Thus began the structuring of the trade as it now exists, with Burgundy, more than any other wine area of France, relying on foreign markets for its customers.

The merchants had often been involved in the wine trade in another form, perhaps as brokers who recognised that more money was to be made in buying and ageing wines for resale, rather than recommending wines in the cellars of the various growers. Louis Lamarosse, the founder of the company now known as Louis Latour, had been Master of the Beaune Guild of Coopers, whilst the early Bouchards had been cloth merchants from the Low Countries, who used to come to Burgundy to sell their woollens in return for wine.

Some of the sales ledgers and correspondence books of this period still survive and it interesting to see how far afield some of the merchants travelled to look out for customers. Though Burgundies had been quite fashionable in England in the seventeenth century, with the Earl of Bedford importing 62 bottles of *Shably* for his cellar at Woburn, the eighteenth century was a bad time for all things French. Already in 1693, Rhenish, Spanish and Portuguese wines paid a lower rate of duty than those from France. The difference became even more marked four years later, when the duty on French wines was raised to £47 2s 10d per tun, whilst those on the wines from the Rhine were only £26 2s 10d per tun. It was a time when popularity could easily be attained by attacking all things French and wines were an easy victim. Queen Anne further increased the duty on French wines to £55 per tun, whilst reducing that on the wines of Britain's ally Portugal to no more than £7. As André Simon said, in a lecture to the Wine Trade Club in 1911,

> However exorbitant the charge for French wines, there was a demand for them so long as the generation of men lasted who had been boys in Charles II's time, but the generations which followed never had the opportunity of appreciating the vintages of France sufficiently to pay the price demanded for these; their consumption gradually decreased almost to vanishing point, and, in that respect, the promoters of the Methuen Treaty attained the object they had in view. It was not, however, solely the increased price at which French wines had to be sold that lost them the favour of the vast majority of wine drinkers in England. The principal cause is to be found in the ceaseless endeavours of politicians, divines, satirists and others to sow and foster throughout the country a most bigoted hatred of the French, and of everything that was French.

That little Burgundy made its way to England is no doubt true, but there must have been some demand for it, or Claude Arnoux would scarcely have had published in London his monograph on the wines of the region in 1728, which was considered important enough to be translated and appear in Philip Miller's *Gardeners' Dictionary*, which appeared shortly afterwards. Entries of customers in England are rare in the sales books of the eighteenth-century Beaune merchants, but they are not totally absent. More common however are entries for the cities of Holland, Germany and the north of France. Pierre Andrieu, in his history of the wines and vineyards of Burgundy, quotes from the correspondence ledgers of some of the early Burgundian merchants. The firm of Gauthey Père et Fils wrote to an agent on 28 August 1783, saying that his letter had taken two weeks to reach them. Customers were to be advised to buy quality wines quickly as prices were rising and it was difficult to find any more. (Somehow the situation has changed little with either the post or the prices!) Apparently the man's horse was worn out, for he was told, 'Try to change it and do not put too high a price upon its head.'

Another old company, Poulet Père et Fils, in 1774 sent out 138 casks of wine to towns which included Danzig, Vienna, Dresden, Munich and Naples. Just one *feuillette* of the total went to Paris. Some of the customers were remarkably loyal to their suppliers: the Chevalier Folard, who first appears in their books in the year 1760, when he was on duty in Munich, sends orders over a span of 35 years. It is noticeable that before the Revolution he regularly included such great wines as Montrachet and Clos de Vougeot in his orders; afterwards he was satisfied with such lesser wines as Passetousgrains.

The mobility of many of these private customers was considerable as often they would be attached to some foreign court in a diplomatic capacity, or to an army fighting on the Rhine or elsewhere. One can only marvel at the delivery service of the day, for wine frequently appears to have been ordered from countries who were at the time at war with France.

With the end of the eighteenth century came the French Revolution and a total change in the structure of vineyard ownership. With the arrival on the market of all the domains that had previously belonged to the nobility and the church, and the introduction of the Napoleonic laws of succession, the fragmentation of the vineyard holdings in Burgundy got rapidly under way — and it has continued to the present day.

Whilst the eighteenth century may have been important in the commercial history of the Burgundy wine trade, the nineteenth was a big period for the improvement in the planting of the vineyards and the making of the wine. It was during this century that the *provignage* system of the regeneration of vines was finally abandoned in favour of the planting of individual vines in rows as we know them at present. The first village to adopt the *taille à cordon Guyot* was Savigny, but the others were soon to follow.

Also, the beginning of the century saw the writings of the Comte Chaptal, who also was to give his name to a current word in the wine world, chaptalisation, or the addition of sugar to the fermenting must in order to increase the alcoholic strength. He originally proposed this technique in order to help the beet-sugar growers of the north of France, who were having difficulty in selling their production. Even in those days there were commodity mountains! Whilst the technique is widespread now, even amongst the finest growers, except perhaps in outstanding vintages, it met with a great deal of criticism when it was first proposed. Indeed, in an enquiry made in 1853, out of 21 Burgundian wine villages consulted, fourteen said that sugaring was unknown amongst their growers and seven said that it might be acceptable in cold years. As the Burgundian writer Vergnette-Lamotte said, at about the same time, in a somewhat withering fashion, 'Chaptal, who was born in the Midi, and, as such, only valued wine by its alcoholic degree, has considered alcohol to be the principal preserving element in wine and it is upon this basis that the sad elements of vinification that govern us today, have been based.'

The major problem of the century in Burgundy, as in most other wine regions of France, was *phylloxera vastatrix*. Though this was first described in the Rhône Valley in 1867, the Burgundians for long thought that it could never happen to them. In 1871, the local authorities had warned everyone to be vigilant, but it was not until July 1878 that a Monsieur Viard discovered the louse in his vines in Meursault. The military were called in and in a rapid operation they claimed to have eradicated the infection for the whole region. Their optimism was short-lived and even though the grafting of French vines on to American rootstock had actually been proposed at a seminar in Beaune on the problems of phylloxera in 1869, the importation of American vines into Burgundy was actually forbidden until a decree of June 1887. In the meantime such companies as Vermorel of Villefranche made their fortune selling their equipment to inject carbon bisulphide into the soil. Even though they could see their vineyards being destroyed in front of their eyes, the Burgundian vineyard owners, for the most part, remained curiously fatalistic. Many believed that the plague would disappear just as easily as it had come. On the other hand, the growers of Puligny led the school that demanded treatment — and, coincidentally, the first wine made from vines grafted onto American rootstocks to win a gold medal at the Paris Wine Fair, was a white Burgundy, a Meursault Goutte d'Or.

Robert Laurent, in *Les Vignerons de la Côte d'Or au XIXe Siecle*, has shown that from the first treatment to final full production again, it took a typical Burgundy fine wine vineyard almost 20 years. The effect on prices, too, was substantial. Le Montrachet leapt by 900 per cent between 1889 and 1891 and the Cuvée Jobard of Meursault Genev-rières from the Hospices de Beaune from 1,060 francs the queue of 470 litres in 1888 to 2,640 in 1891. For many growers the cost of replanting proved too much. Maurice Fondet has estimated it at 4,000 francs per hectare on the properties of the Hospices de Beaune. They could afford this, because their vineyards were spread along the Côte de Beaune and not all attacked at once. In addition, they were well endowed and could find the necessary money from their reserves. Few were so lucky. The area under vines in the Beaune region fell from 28,000 hectares in 1875 to 13,000 in 1897. If one considers that these were vineyards, for the most part, which sold expensive wine and were thus worth replanting, one can only imagine what the situation was like in more marginal areas. Almost overnight, the vineyard area in Burgundy halved, much of it never to be replanted. The areas which suffered particularly were the vineyards of the Yonne, until then the most extensive in Burgundy, the Arrières-Côtes and some of those of the Côte Chalonnaise.

The situation for the growers went from bad to worse at the beginning of the century. Those who had invested a fortune in replanting their vineyards now found it difficult to sell their wines and prices fell just as quickly as they had risen. At the Hospices de Beaune sale of 1900, all but one of the white wine cuvées sold for less than a third of the price that the previous vintage had fetched — and it was not until the sale of 1906 that there was to be any significant increase in the prices paid.

The reasons for this crisis are not totally clear. A combi-nation of reasons seems to have been involved. Of these perhaps the most important was the vast increase in production after the replanting of the vineyards. Charles Gide, in a speech that he made in Paris in May 1900, foresaw the problem when he said, 'Each hectare that has been replanted, represents, as a productive power, three or four times as much as each hectare that was grubbed up.' It also appears that during the crisis, many of the growers made 'artificial' wines from grape juice and sugar for their own consumption. Some of these reached the market and there was a general disillusion in France with the drinking of wine. It became fashionable amongst the richer families to drink either tea or beer.

It was during the nineteenth century, too, that the Chardonnay finally established itself as the great white wine grape of Burgundy, though more often than not it was considered as the same variety as the Pinot Blanc. In the survey of 1853 already mentioned, all those who answered the questionnaire stated that they considered this grape to be the best for fine wines. As far as ordinary white wine was concerned feelings appear to have been split between the Plant de Troyes or Aligoté, and the Melon. What is interesting to note is that it was widely held, until the middle of the century, that grapes owed their characteristics to the climate, rather than to any individual characteristics they might have. Thus any white grape planted in Burgundy would tend to make the same style of wine, though there might be some minor variations in both quantity and quality. It is apparent then, that, for many centuries, there had not generally been ideal vines for any particular region. Many varieties had grown side by side.

The twentieth century has seen many improvements to all levels of wine-making. Treatments are now generally available to protect the vines against the series of problems that might beset them, be they animal, fungal or climatic. There have also been developments in the press-house and the cellar. The old hand press is of the past and the Vaslin is now being overtaken by the Willmes. The use of stainless steel and temperature control at the time of fermentation is certainly giving wines that are fresher and have more apparent fruit.

They are not the wines of the past, that is certain; whether they are as great as those wines of the past is a matter of opinion. It is fair to say, though, that there are far fewer bad wines than there were. A disastrous vintage, as far as quality is concerned, is a thing of the past.

It is fashionable to say, perhaps more of red Burgundies than of white, that the wines are not what they used to be. Wines, even in such a traditional region as Burgundy, are moulded by the requirements of the consumer. Whilst there are a certain small number of producers who try to impose their style, their number is decreasing. No one can say for certain what a young white Burgundy of, say, the early 1900s might have tasted like. There is little doubt that it would have been fuller in body and deeper in colour. In certain cases it is also likely that it would have been slightly sweet.

Commercial demand has meant that white Burgundy is drunk, and made to be drunk, much younger than it was in the past. Long ageing in cask, followed by storage in bottle, is expensive and seems to be unnecessary as far as the consumer is concerned. Youth is accepted; indeed many drinkers have not had the opportunity of tasting old white Burgundies. Largely it is a matter of taste, but financially, for the producer and even the retailer, it is a taste that makes good commercial sense.

Recent years have seen fluctuations in price just as dramatic as those at the turn of the century. For all the developments that there have been over the centuries, no one has yet managed to match the supply of white Burgundy with the demand for it. World markets are expanding all the time. The expansion of white wine production has been note-worthy, too, over the past fifteen years. It will never be easy to guarantee total success in Burgundy either in the field of commerce or of quality, for there are too many outside influences. In both fields, however, the future looks bright. But the picture of the white wines of Burgundy is a constantly changing pattern. Herein lies its interest.

3
The Burgundy Factors

The construction of a fine wine is not a simple process. It depends on a number of circumstances coming together at the right time and in the right place. Of these circumstances, some are permanent, or at least unchangeable, like the soil and the weather (though it must be said that in both these cases, man is doing his best to alter them to suit his own purposes). Others are variable, such as the variety of grape that is used for making the wine, the treatments of both the vine and the wine, and, in some ways the most important of all, the man that oversees the production.

Wine, at least in Burgundy, is not a stereotyped product that comes off a factory line in unlimited quantities and of unvarying quality. There is little doubt that modern techniques are enabling more, and possibly better, wine to be made, but, for example, great wines cannot generally be made after poor summers and autumns. Similarly, to make fine wine demands dedication on the part of the grower. Whilst some have sought to cut corners by increasing production, by over-fertilising their vines, planting clones that give big yields, or by failing to prune when necessary, there are as many who have realised that for the wines of Burgundy to command the high prices that are being asked for them, the quality should be controlled as much as possible.

Of these factors, which is the most important? Dr Jules Guyot, who conducted a detailed study of viticulture in the northerly vineyards of France for the Ministry of Agriculture in 1866, had little doubt. He wrote, 'The essence of the great wines of the Côte d'Or is the grape variety; it is the Pinot

Noir or Noirien for the red wines, it is the Pinot Blanc or Chardonnay for the white wines.' It must be recognised that Dr Guyot was writing in circumstances different from those that apply today. The major problem of Burgundy was still the widespread planting of grape varieties for their yield rather than for their quality. Particularly serious was the overwhelming proportion of Gamay that was still planted in many of the greatest red wine vineyards of Burgundy, and, to a lesser extent, the Aligoté or the Plant de Troyes, for the making of white wines. Whilst the growers recognised the quality advantage of the Pinot Noir and the Chardonnay, they chose to follow the path of quantity. Interestingly, in the 1853 questionnaire mentioned in the last chapter, the first question was, 'What variety should be chosen for making ordinary wine?' All the 27 villages had an answer. However, to the second question, 'What variety should be chosen for making fine wine?', four of them surprisingly could find no answer.

Dr Guyot carries on, 'It is thus to its choice of grape variety, that the Côte d'Or owes most of all its great reputation; but it is not just to this choice of Pinot Noir and Blanc that this reputation is due, it is to its oneness. The Pinot, since the seventh century, has *by itself* created the great wines of Burgundy.' Indeed it is true today that Burgundy, unlike most of the other great wines of France, is nearly always made from one grape variety, and that if it is a great white Burgundy, that grape variety will be the Chardonnay.

The separation into distinct personalities of the Pinot Blanc and the Chardonnay is a recent event. Alexis Lichine in his *Wines of France*, which appeared first in 1952, talks of the Pinot Chardonnay, as it was then generally known. Indeed, there is still the appellation Pinot-Chardonnay-Mâcon, for the white wines from that region, even though the regulations state that the wines can be made 'either from the Pinot Blanc or the Chardonnay'. Nevertheless the Chardonnay is now one of the great grapes of worldwide reputation for the making of white wines, whilst the Pinot Blanc's reputation seems to be on the downward slope.

There is a village called Chardonnay in the Mâconnais and it is probable that the grape variety takes its name from this unassuming place which boasts little more than a co-operative cellar and 200 inhabitants. As a vine it is particularly suited to the limestone soil that is present in so much of Burgundy and its plantings have increased quite considerably over the past 20 years. The reasons for this are twofold. First, there has been an enormous increase in the demand for white wines, and specially those of Burgundy, spearheaded by the American consumer. Secondly, new plantings in Burgundy are restricted to those areas where there have traditionally been vines. The areas that have until recently remained unplanted have been those that have lain fallow since the phylloxera plague at the end of the last century, like Chablis and the Arrière-Côtes of the Côte d'Or, or since the First World War, like the Côte Chalonnaise. In all these three cases, the soil is well adapted to the planting of the Chardonnay — and the growers recently have not been slow to profit from it.

At present, some 15 per cent of the Burgundy vineyards are planted in Chardonnay, which in terms of production leaves it a poor third to the Gamay and the Pinot Noir. This area represents, in all, about 5,600 hectares, of which more than half is in the Saône et Loire *département*. The rapid increase in the production of Chablis is dealt with elsewhere, but it is very interesting to note that the area under vines there has almost quadrupled during the last 40 years, with the real expansion coming in the last 15.

What are the advantages of the Chardonnay as the grape variety? First, and most importantly, it produces wines that appeal to the consumer, whether they are aged in small oak casks like the finest Meursaults or in stainless steel, like many Chablis and the wines of the Mâconnais. Secondly, it is not a timid variety. It grows easily and abundantly, producing wines comparatively high in alcohol. However, its resistance to mildew is no more than average and it suffers equally from other forms of rot. One particular problem that one can see in Burgundy regularly is *court noué*, known in English as fan-leaf, a viral disease which affects the whole vine, and of which the one symptom that is easily visible is a paling of the leaves.

As Burgundy is a northerly vineyard area, all the grape varieties used must be early ripening. The Chardonnay is no exception. Early ripening also means early shooting and a regular problem is spring frosts, most particularly in the Chablis vineyards.

The Chardonnay, then, is responsible for producing all the great white wines of Burgundy, from Chablis, from the Côte d'Or, from the Côte Chalonnaise and from the Mâconnais. Indeed, legislation does not permit the use of any other variety, including the Pinot Blanc, in the making of either Chablis or Pouilly-Fuissé. The success that it has had in giving the white wines of Burgundy their greatness, has led to its being planted in just about every country where wine is made, even in such exotic locations as India, where it is used in the production of local 'Champagne'. That its supply in Burgundy itself is unable to meet demand has led one major company, Louis Latour, to have made more plantings in the Ardèche *département*.

If the star of the Chardonnay is in the ascendant, that of the Pinot Blanc is definitely on the decline. One has the impression that it had a great reputation whilst it was confused with the Chardonnay, but that now that it is recognised as being a distinct creature, and not even a relative, it has great difficulty in creating an image for itself. Indeed, it is impossible to have any clear idea of how much is now planted in Burgundy, and I know of few who claim to vinify it by itself. Even in Alsace, where a great deal of wine is made and sold as Pinot Blanc, most of it is now made from the Auxerrois, which is yet another distinct grape variety, with its origins in Lorraine. In Alsace, much of it is used for the production of sparkling wines, because of its rather neutral taste. It is possible therefore that its plantings in Burgundy could be increased, with this specific use in mind.

Another member of the Pinot family that is still grown in Burgundy is the Pinot Gris, which is known locally as the Pinot Beurot. Historically, it was planted widely in the red wine vineyards, as it was thought that a proportion of its grapes in the vat added finesse to the wine. The Viscount de Vergnette claims that such wines would be made up to an eighth of white grapes in the mixture and that many oenologists of the time, the end of the eighteenth century, regretted the passing of this habit as it gave to the wines, 'éclat, delicacy, vivacity and keeping qualities'. It seems that the habit of making deeply coloured red wines came in with the vintage of 1795, which were at first severely criticised abroad, but soon came to be accepted as the norm. Amongst local producers there were many who fought against this trend unsuccessfully. Even now there are two opposing factions in the ranks of Burgundy lovers, those who prefer full-bodied, deep-coloured red wines, and those who prefer them with rather more delicacy and, perhaps, less colour.

Historically, also, the Pinot Beurot had another role in the wines of Burgundy. It was used for the making of *vin de paille*, a sweet dessert wine, which now only seems to be made on a commercial but minute scale in the vineyards of the Jura.

Wine made from the Pinot Beurot, by itself, tends to be rather high in alcohol and much lower in apparent acidity than the Chardonnay. It gives a full-bodied, discreet flavour which is appreciated by those who are comparative new-comers to the white wines of Burgundy. The wines should generally be drunk young, as they tend to oxidise rather more quickly than most Burgundies. Another problem is that the grapes are particularly sensitive to fungal diseases, though, on the other hand, the vines are resistant to frost damage. It is rarely found in Burgundy and can be more readily appreci-ated as the Pinot Gris — Tokay d'Alsace, in that area.

The Pinot Gris is still occasionally to be found planted amongst red wine vines, and, in effect, it has, as a grape, a broad range of presentations, from the almost white to the almost black. It is vinified rarely by itself, though I do know of three growers in the Hautes-Côtes de Beaune who offer their customers a Pinot Beurot white wine.

In terms of planting, the second most popular white grape in Burgundy is the Aligoté, though as a proportion of the total production it is in steady decline. It covers about 3 per cent of the total vineyard area. Yet again, it is a variety that has suffered changing fortunes over the years. Even though the area under this grape has decreased in the past 30 years, due to improved techniques production has increased from about 36,000 hectolitres each year to a current total of something over 45,000 hectolitres.

The grower who has been making wine from the Aligoté, which can be sold as nothing more pretentious than Bourgogne Aligoté, has been on a roller-coaster ride as far as profits are concerned. One of the more interesting features of Hugh Johnson's first *World Atlas of Wine*, which appeared in 1971, is a breakdown of the accounts of growers making a number of different wines in Burgundy. All but one were making a return on their investment; the exception was the producer of Bourgogne Aligoté. In the third edition, which appeared in 1985, the same tables are given. Now the Aligoté producer is making a reasonable return; a higher one in fact than the grower in Clos Vougeot or in Richebourg. In her recent book, *Vines, Grapes and Wines*, Jancis Robinson says, 'In the old days, much white wine from Burgundy was a blend of Aligoté, Chardonnay and perhaps some Pinot Blanc and Melon. Since the introduction of Appellation Controlée laws, such commingling is not allowed and wine made from Aligoté must be sold (and ostracised) as Bourgogne Aligoté, at around half the price of a Bourgogne Blanc made from Chardonnay. The yield of Aligoté may be better than that of Chardonnay but it certainly is not the double needed to compensate financially.'

It is true that in the old days, the Aligoté was quite regularly blended in with the finer wines, and this was taken as a matter of course in many villages. Indeed, when the laws were drawn up from the *appellation controlée* of Corton-Charlemagne and Charlemagne in 1937 it is apparent that there must have been quite considerable plantings of Aligoté in the two vineyards, as the decree states, 'However, the Aligoté will be forbidden for all new and replacement plantings from 1938 and must be replaced by the Pinot Chardonnay before 1948.' No such exemption was given for le Montrachet!

When Jancis talks about the poor return of Aligoté plantations, she is some years out of date. As so many vines have been rooted up, makers of this wine have found that the only way for demand to be curtailed to meet supply is by the simple expedient of raising prices. As I write this, the price-lists from Burgundy are offering Bourgogne Aligoté at a higher price than they are quoting for Mâcon-Villages, made from the Chardonnay. It is a moot point as to whether these prices truly represent the intrinsic merits of the two wines, but, nevertheless, they reflect what the customer is prepared to pay at this moment. One factor that has helped increase the standing of the Aligoté is the creation, in March 1979, of the new appellation Bourgogne Aligoté Bouzeron, for wines produced in that commune, for this, for the first time, has personalised a wine made from the Aligoté grape.

The Aligoté, which is the same grape as the Plant de Troyes mentioned earlier as being recommended by nineteenth-century growers as best for making ordinary white wines, has a number of advantages as a variety. Of these, perhaps the two most important are that it ripens early and has a notably higher yield than the Chardonnay. In Burgundy it is mainly grown on the fringe of Chablis and the Côte Chalonnaise, the Arrières-Côtes and in one or two villages of the Côte d'Or, those with the best reputations coming perhaps from Puligny-Montrachet and Pernand-Vergelesses. Aligoté is also widely used for sparkling wines.

Finally, there are two grape-varieties which are permitted for the production of certain wines; the Melon, for the most basic Bourgogne Grand Ordinaire, throughout Burgundy, and the Sacy, for making Bourgogne, just in the Yonne *département*. The Melon as a grape has succeeded more as an exile than it has in its native land. It is a poor cousin of the Pinot family, which has now created its finest reputation in the production of Muscadet. In Burgundy, Galet states that there are something over 600 hectares still in production, mostly in the Saône et Loire *département*, but this compares with the 9,000 hectares in Muscadet. The resultant wine is somewhat high in acidity and short lived. Burgundian chefs claim that it is ideal for sauces as it does not colour them. Coincidentally, the Chardonnay is known as the Melon Blanc in Arbois.

Sacy is the name of not just a grape, but also of a village in the Chablis area. As a grape, it is probably the last of the white grapes to survive from a host of large-yielding varieties which contributed half the total production of the Yonne *département* until phylloxera struck in the latter half of the nineteenth century. In 1935, Albert Pic says that it was used for the 'ordinary wines to which have been given the appellation "Bourgogne des Environs de Chablis"'. In fact, this simple statement hides a long battle fought by the producers of Chablis to protect the quality of their name, by restricting its production to wines made from the Chardonnay, or Beaunois, as it is known in the region.

I have only tasted one Bourgogne made from pure Sacy, from the house of Laroche. It appears that most of the wine now made from the Sacy, because of its low degree in alcohol and comparatively high degree of acidity, is used for the production of sparkling wine. Nevertheless in good years it makes an agreeably refreshing light wine.

The above grapes are those that are used for the production of *appellation controlée* wines. Some non-appellation wine is still made, particularly in the plain of the Saône, but more distinctive is the white V.D.Q.S. wine still made close to Chablis. This is the Sauvignon de Saint Bris, which comes from the village of the same name, and some of its neighbours. No one seems clear when this variety came to be planted, but it is probable that it came from Sancerre, which is nearer to Saint Bris than the majority of the Côte d'Or vineyards, some time during the nineteenth century. The wine received official recognition in 1974 and there are less than 60 hectares of the vine planted.

The importance of soil as a quality factor in the production of fine wines is one that has been widely discussed recently. Bill Jekel, who owns vineyards in the richly fertile Salinas Valley of California, is the leading protagonist of the school that believes that soil is only of secondary importance. Certainly, by French standards, the soil of his vineyards could be considered too opulent for the production of great wines, yet he has managed to show that he is capable of producing wines from neighbouring vines, which can rival the best from both Bordeaux and Burgundy, in red and white. Whatever Mr Jekel might believe, tradition in Burgundy states that the finest white wines in Burgundy come from those vineyards where there is a noticeable proportion of chalk in the soil, which drain well and which are on the slopes to give some protection against frost damage.

In *Terroirs et Vins de France*, edited by Charles Pomerol, the authors have little doubt of these three essentials. As they say of the Côte d'Or,

> Thus plain A.C. Bourgogne vineyards are generally situated on land at the bottom of the slopes, where for the most part the slope is less than two per cent, whilst the village A.C.'s and those of the *crus* prosper on slopes from three to five per cent, or even as high as twenty per cent in the case of the *grands crus* of Corton for example.
>
> The fact that the proportion of stones in the soil varies from five to forty per cent in the village appellations and the *crus*, whilst it is generally below five per cent in plain Bourgogne, is of great significance. This 'stoniness' is essential as far as quality is concerned, because of the role that it plays in the dampness factor of the soil: facility of drainage and limitation of excessive water retention . . .
>
> Proportions of total chalk, which vary from nought to fifty per cent, can be found throughout the soils, but low values (less than ten per cent) are most frequent in the low-lying vineyards with no more than regional appellations.

The same source stresses that the finest vineyards of the Chablis region are restricted to those vineyards where the rocky soil is mainly the chalky marl known as Kimmeridgian, after the small village of Kimmeridge in Dorset, where it can also be found.

Whilst it can be said that the best vineyards are those that are on slopes, there is little doubt that one of the strong points of the vineyards of the Côte d'Or is that they are on slopes that face, for the most part, in an easterly direction. The advantages are twofold. By facing east, the vine receives the first rays of the rising sun and thus reaches optimum ripening temperature early in the day — and maintains it. Secondly, in Burgundy, the predominant rain-bearing winds are westerlies and the hills of the Morvan to the west cause much of the rain to fall before the crucial belt of vineyards is reached.

To make fine wines, the correct climatic conditions are necessary. For a perfect vintage, the ideal years would have a mild, but rather wet spring, with no severe, or more particularly late frosts, at the time of first growth; good weather at the time of flowering, so that the fruit can set; a hot summer, with periods of gentle rain, and certainly not severe storms with hail, which can strip a vineyard and damage the fruit. Finally, the autumn should be warm and fine, until the vintage is over. Lying not far from the northern limits of the vine, Burgundy cannot rely on these in every year. It is not California, where the summers are regularly fine and the autumns long and warm, where irrigation can replace any shortage in rainfall in just the proportions that are needed. Far too often, what has been declared as a great vintage at the end of a fine summer, has become no more than an average one as a result of a very wet autumn. However it must be pointed out that the effects of the weather tend to be rather less with white wines than with red, because the rot which can destroy a red wine, if the mould infected grapes are not totally discarded before vatting, has less effect on white wines, where the skins are discarded immediately after pressing. There tend to be fewer extremes in the quality of the white wines of Burgundy, than there are with the reds.

What is it that makes the difference between the excellent wines of a vineyard, like le Montrachet, and a very good one, like its neighbour Puligny Caillerets? They both lie on the same level on the slope and at their extremities, there is just a path that separates them. Individual wines might benefit or suffer from the care taken by the grower and the man who makes and tends the wine. Over the centuries, the reputations of the two wines have been well divided. Le Montrachet must have that position on the slope that is ideal to gain the maximum benefit from the sun. It must have that vein of something special in the soil that gives the wine those particular characteristics that have made it stand out in an area of outstanding white wines.

Whilst the grapes, the climate and the soil all have an important effect on the quality of any wine, it is ultimately in the hands of the man who makes the wine as to whether it is good or great. Carelessness on his part can quite easily spoil the finest wine. He has to decide when the grapes should be picked and delay can spoil everything. Often it is rains at vintage time that turn a great vintage into a poor one. Whilst rot is less important for white wines than for red, the flavour of the wine can be spoiled if rotten grapes are not rejected. Too much sun can also be a problem, though this is a rarer occurrence. In 1983, though, overripe white grapes caused problems for many growers, who were unable to ferment their wines out fully, and, even if they achieved this, often found that the wines lacked the necessary acidity to hold them together.

The pressing of grapes is now done almost totally in horizontal presses. The Vaslin horizontal screw-press is now the most common in Burgundy, but there are many white wine producers who now prefer the Willmes pneumatic press, as they feel that the flavour of the fruit is better preserved, as there is less chance of unattractive traces being crushed out of the pips. The pneumatic press is gentler in its operation.

Historically, the fermentation of white wines in Burgundy has taken place in the cask. The grapes arrive from the vineyard, they are pressed and the juice passed straight into cask for fermentation. Now, often for reasons of economy and space, the fermentation takes place in vats. The whole question of both fermentation and ageing in wood or vat is discussed elsewhere in this book, but there is little doubt that the style of many white Burgundies has changed radically over the past few years, because many producers have decided to do without casks at both stages in a wine's life. Whilst I might agree that there is little to be gained by fermenting white wines in cask, I am certain that great white Burgundies, and these include the better Chablis, gain from spending some time in small oak casks. Many wines, particularly from those villages like Pouilly-Fuissé and Meursault, which produce fuller-bodied wine, benefit from spending at least part of their life in new oak casks. With the prices that are now being paid for the white wines of Burgundy, there is no reason why a grower cannot afford to buy some new casks each vintage. Oak is what gives polish to a wine.

The time of bottling is also important when the final style of a wine is to be considered. It is largely correct to say that the greater a wine is, the later it should be bottled. However, another important factor is the ultimate style that the producer seeks. White Burgundies are often criticised by New World winemakers as being oxidised. This might be partly as a result of being kept in cask too long before bottling, or more seriously, because of unhygienic cellar techniques. However the European, and particularly, the Englishman, does not always look for the same attributes in his dry white wine. Americans tend to drink them young; the Englishman often prefers them older — and rounded.

The French, too, seem to have an abhorrence of white Burgundies with much age. Even *grands crus* they seem to appreciate most when they are just two or three years old. This is illustrated by the fact that when I worked in France, I spent much of my time trying to sell to the finest restaurants in Paris and elsewhere. The company for which I worked still had a number of wines from Corton Charlemagne on its list, which were from great vintages ten or more years old. According to the textbooks, this is the ideal age for a great white Burgundy, but they were rejected by the French as being far too old. On the other hand, they were all greedily absorbed by the British market.

For the American, and the Frenchman, freshness and crispness are the two main attributes looked for in a white Burgundy. The English consumer, if given the chance, will happily enjoy a wine that has been given time to develop its secondary flavours. Perhaps the greater extremes of climate in the United States preclude the greater ageing of white Burgundies. The American is happy with what he receives, young wine, and is not prepared to seek any further.

It has to be realised that the making of any great wine depends on three factors; what is there from nature: the climate, the soil and the exposure of the vineyard; what is there from man: the selection of grape variety, the method of pruning, of making and of ageing the wine; and what is there by law. Each area has its own traditions as to what is permitted. The Burgundian might chaptalise his wines, whilst the Californian is not allowed to. On the other hand the Californian might irrigate his vines, a practice forbidden in Burgundy. To many over-chaptalisation is the habit which does most to spoil the wines of Burgundy, though this is often more apparent in the red wines than in the whites. The fact that the habit is permitted in every vintage leads many makers to feel that it is now a necessity in Burgundy, rather than a useful possibility.

Is chaptalisation a necessity in Burgundy, or is it a convenience that is too often abused? The truth must lie somewhere between the two. It is true that Burgundy is one of the most northerly vineyard areas in the world and, as such, has difficulty, in many years, in making good wines without recourse to additional sugar. In an ideal world, I am sure that most people would be happier if wine were made totally naturally, without any additional ingredients. However, this would mean that there would be much less drinkable wine on the market, and prices would inevitably rise.

The fact is that chaptalisation, for too many growers, is an easy way out. The legal limits are often abused and, in certain cases, most particularly with regard to wines from the Beaujolais, the style of the wine may be altered. Now, even in the best years, when the climatic conditions have been ideal, some growers will, nevertheless, chaptalise. In Bordeaux, for example, the process is only permitted in certain years. Could this be a possibility for Burgundy? As an alternative, chaptalisation might be forbidden for all wines of, say, *premier cru* status and above. Realistically, however, it is difficult to see how the Burgundians would sacrifice such a convenience. For my part, I would be satisfied if the excesses were controlled, and if the laws about chaptalisation were applied more firmly. It would be interesting, also, if some growers were to make over a range of vintages, chaptalised and unchaptalised wines in parallel. Then we would really know what effect it had on the quality.

It is the individuality of its wines which gives Burgundy its eminent position in the world vinous hierarchy. This individuality stems from two sources. The first is the obstinacy of the Burgundian grower in preferring to make smaller quantities of a large number of wines — and it must be accepted that whilst there might be more work in pursuing this policy, there is also much more money to be made. The second is the infinite variety of the ingredients that go to make the final product. While much is controlled by the wine laws, much more is left to the individual. It is the coming together of all these different quality factors that leads to the final product, called by many the finest white wine in the world — Burgundy.

4
The Generic Burgundies

The fact has to be faced that those white wines of Burgundy about which we talk the most are now expensive. Whilst we enjoy our bottles of Puligny and Meursault, Chablis and Pouilly-Fuissé, we cannot afford to drink them every day. Price, for most of us, is a limiting factor. Are there alternatives more reasonably priced within Burgundy? The answer has to be a guarded, 'Yes'. At the bottom of the range of Burgundian appellations there are white wines to be found, but even their prices have been dragged higher by the success of their more illustrious relatives.

I feel that whoever created the hierarchy of wine names in Burgundy must have lacked imagination. Whatever the quality might be of the least white wine of the region, it seems sad that no more exciting name could be found for it than Bourgogne Ordinaire, and *ordinaire* in French is directly translatable as *ordinary* in English. Whilst the wine might occasionally be ordinary, it seems poor marketing to describe it as such. Agreed, there is the alternative Bourgogne Grand Ordinaire, but this seems to add insult to injury. There is no more merit in describing a wine as 'very ordinary' rather than just 'ordinary'.

In effect, white Bourgogne Grand Ordinaire can be made from just one, or a blend, of all the permitted white grapes in Burgundy; that is to say such regulars as the Chardonnay and the Aligoté, and such historical relics as the Melon de Bourgogne and, in the Yonne *département*, the Sacy. These last two, particularly, have largish yields of rather acid, neutral wines; wines that are ideal for turning into the local sparkler Crémant de Bourgogne. As sales of this fluctuate considerably, depending on the cost of Champagne (it sells when Champagne is expensive and is much more a regional speciality when Champagne is cheap), the possibility of being able to make Bourgogne Grand Ordinaire as an alternative is attractive.

As opposed to all the other white wines of Burgundy, that of B.G.O., as its is commonly known, has declined dramatically. The total production now, in an average year, is 2,400 hectolitres. To put this in perspective, the production of the single *grand cru* vineyard Corton Charlemagne, at 1,300 hectolitres is over half as much. The fact that the popularity of this wine has suffered first from its name, and secondly from alternative uses for the grapes, is just part of the whole problem. Even more important is the fact that to plant a vineyard to make specifically this wine makes little sense. On it, you might just as well plant Chardonnay to make Bourgogne, or even Aligoté, to make Bourgogne Aligoté. The returns on both of these are distinctly greater. It is true to say that much of the B.G.O. came from what were considered marginal vineyards owned by part-time vignerons. With the current prices for Burgundies, such a condition scarcely exists.

Whether the appellation should still exist is another problem. One has only to look at one like Charlemagne, which has not been produced for a generation, but which is still on the record books, to understand how hard it would be to suppress it. Vested interests are hard to overcome in Burgundy. Where do those vested interests lie? Who now makes Bourgogne Grand Ordinaire? As far as the white wines are concerned, there remain just two small areas where it is produced in reasonable but small quantities. Of these, one is on the fringes of the Chablis region and the other is on the Côte Chalonnaise. Significantly, both these are now centres of the production of sparkling wine. In the Chablis region, one grower who still makes a little of the wine, mainly from the Sacy grape, is Roland Viré, at Chitry. On the Côte Chalonnaise, where the wine will be based upon the Melon de Bourgogne, the grape that more notably is Muscadet, production seems to be centred on the co-operative cellar at Buxy, which in the better years makes most enjoyable wines. Nevertheless, as the total production of the appellation has dropped by 75 per cent in the last fifteen years or so, one does not need to be clairvoyant to predict its future. Interestingly, in the summer of 1987, murmurs started coming out of Burgundy as to the eventual suppression of this appellation. It will be interesting to see whether there is any impetus behind this move.

On the next rung of the hierarchial scale comes the appellation Bourgogne Aligoté. It is not too long ago that the same fate was being predicted for this wine as for B.G.O. Somehow, and it is not very easy to see why, the Aligoté grape, from which the wine is made, though Chardonnay may also be added, sems to have fought off its attackers and stabilised its position. Once again it is used widely for the production of sparkling wines, but Bourgogne Aligoté as a wine in its own right seems to be finding a larger market, to such an extent that its price has been nudging that asked for some Chardonnay wines. It would be pleasant to think that this was because certain wines made from the Aligoté are better than certain wines made from the Chardonnay. This may be true, though the Chardonnay inherently makes a better wine than the Aligoté. The fact is that it is the old law of supply and demand coming into effect. Less Aligoté has been planted at a time of crisis for the wine. The crisis has now passed and it has recreated for itself a certain fashionable following.

It might be that its role as the traditional ingredient as the wine needed to make a Kir has had a part in this renaissance, for the Burgundian aperitif now appears to have achieved a following in the smarter bars and restaurants in London and New York, as well as Paris. Another contributing factor must have been the creation in 1979 of the grape's first geographical appellation, Bourgogne Aligoté Bouzeron. One notable result of this was that the grape immediately gained more credibility, and a higher price. Whilst there may not have been much forethought going into the creation of some of the wine names of Burgundy, this one was conceived in a very commercial fashion.

It is interesting to think why Bouzeron particularly should have been selected for this individual honour. True, it has for long had a reputation for its wines made from the Aligoté. But then, so have such villages as Puligny-Montrachet and Pernand-Vergelesses, on the Côte d'Or, Bouze-les-Beaune in the Hautes-Côtes and, for that matter, Chitry-le-Fort and Saint-Bris in the Yonne. Perhaps it was to honour this small village on the Côte Chalonnaise, which has had a long vinous history. Perhaps it is more in honour of some of the famous names who own vines there. To me it appears a dangerous precedent, for having granted the appellation to one village, it must be more difficult to refuse it to another. Whilst the wines of Bouzeron might be excellent in their particular field, there are others at the same level of equal merit.

The Bourgogne Aligoté is grown less widely than it was, but it can be found throughout Burgundy. For example, the village of Puligny-Montrachet has almost 50 hectares planted with this vine, on the flat land to the east of the main road, between it and the railway line. Henri Cannard has said of these wines, 'Situated on excellent white wine soil, these Bourgogne Aligotés are of outstanding quality. They produce a type of wine that escapes from the normal for this variety to have more depth, more roundness, more body. They approach wines produced from the Chardonnay; less acidity, but the taste is typified by the soil it comes from'.

The other Côte d'Or village particularly noted for making excellent Aligotés is Pernand-Vergelesses. Here the vines are not planted on the plain, for the village has none, but rather on the slopes behind the village. This gives the wines a certain finesse that is often lacking. This is enhanced when the grower adds in a proportion of Chardonnay, as I feel certain must be the case with one of my favourites, Dubreuil-Fontaine.

Over the past few years, the Yonne also seems to have built up a fine reputation for not just its wines from Chablis, but also its Aligotés, often from just outside the Chablis area. In Saint-Bris, many of the growers are abandoning the local speciality, the Sauvignon, in favour of the Aligoté — once again there is the fall-back position of being sparkling material. Local merchants, too, like Lamblin and Laroche, are building up their markets for this wine.

One area where there has been a decline in the production of Bourgogne Aligoté is the Hautes-Côtes. Since they were given their personal regional names in 1961, the growers have tended to pull up their Aligoté and replant with Chardonnay or even Pinot Beurot for their white wines, as the returns are better. Much Aligoté is also produced on the Côte Chalonnaise, even on such properties as Château de Davenay at Buxy, which for its Chardonnays has the right to the appellation Montagny.

Ideally, a Bourgogne Aligoté is a wine that should be drunk young — almost a white wine equivalent of a Beaujolais. Indeed some restaurants make a feature of drawing it straight from the cask and serving it from a pitcher. Even at its best, it cannot be termed a great wine, but it has a rustic charm. Often, in the years when sunshine has been at a premium, its acidity comes as something of a surprise to the drinker. The answer, in such circumstances, is to add a fifth as much again of Crème de Cassis liqueur, just enough to counteract the acidity; the response a *vin blanc cassis* or Kir.

Bourgogne Aligoté is a wine without pretensions, but yet again it is a wine — and we will meet many of them in this book — which, because of market forces, is in danger of selling itself too dearly. It is good news that the decline in its production has been halted — but it is never a Chardonnay.

A wine that almost always is a Chardonnay is the plain Bourgogne. Once again, those responsible for this wine's christening have got it wrong. In the vineyards of Bordeaux, the lowest of all wines is called simply Bordeaux, and one knows what to expect when one buys a bottle. In Burgundy, one would therefore expect the simplest wine to be called, simply, Bourgogne. This is not the case. Bourgogne is already on the third step of the ladder and has to be made from the best grape varieties available, effectively the Chardonnay, but occasionally, the Pinot Beurot or the Pinot Blanc. The price that is asked for such a wine has to reflect its quality. Would it not be much more logical to rename Bourgogne Grand Ordinaire, Bourgogne; keep Bourgogne Aligoté as it is and upgrade Bourgogne to something more worthy of its image, like Bourgogne Supérieur? One of the current anomalies is that, in Britain, you can label a wine House Burgundy, with just the official appellation of Bourgogne Grand Ordinaire. Yet, in theory at least, Bourgogne means Burgundy — and vice versa, so whilst Bourgogne Grand Ordinaire is two levels lower as an appellation than Bourgogne, it can quite legally be described here by Bourgogne's English translation, Burgundy.

The big advantage of the appellation Bourgogne is that it is generally the source for the branded Burgundies sold by the big wine merchants. Thus a wine like Cuvée Latour, Leroy d'Auvenay or Cuvée Alexis Chanson will have the *appellation controlée* Bourgogne. Latour, Leroy and Chanson can find sources for their wines throughout Burgundy, which gives them a great deal of flexibility when it comes to constructing the blend.

There are two main sources for Bourgogne *tout court*. The first and perhaps the most important is from those vineyards which have the right to a higher appellation, but choose not to use it. Thus, much of the wine from the Mâcon Villages, for example, is declassified to reappear in the merchants' Burgundy blends. The demand is there and the customer is prepared to pay the price. Not very long ago, some of the lesser villages of the Côte de Beaune would also similarly declassify their wines. Nowadays the demand for such wines as Saint-Romain and Auxey-Duresses has increased to such an extent that they sell without difficulty under their own name at higher prices.

The second source is from those vineyards which have right to no better name than just Bourgogne. Amongst these may be some which enjoy a great reputation in their own right. The Château de Meursault vineyard of André Boisseaux is one example of this. The land falls outside the area with right to the appellation of the village. Similarly, most of the villages of the Côte d'Or have a broad band of vines, towards the plain, which produces nothing higher rated than Bourgogne. This is particularly true of the three great white wine villages of Meursault, Puligny and Chassagne. In each case the wines tend to have the characteristics of the individual village, but lacking somewhat the concentration of those characteristics. There are also considerable areas within Burgundy, in villages whose names may never appear on a label, where Bourgogne is produced. Some of these have been given their own special sub-appellations, like the Hautes-Côtes de Nuits and Beaune for their wines, red, white and rosé, or Marsannay for its rosé and Irancy for its red wines. However, outside these areas, there are quite considerable vineyards, which escape any other appellation.

Given the diversity of its sources, it is impossible to say what a Bourgogne blanc might taste like. At its best, it can be the equal of many 'village' wines and in such cases can sell as expensively. More commonly, though, it is a classic Chardonnay, which is likely to have spent little or no time in cask. It should represent the best value for money for the drinker who cannot afford a great wine from the region, but finds it impossible to live without the idea.

5
Chablis and the Yonne

I am in the process of developing a theory that goes something like this, 'The due reputation of a wine is in inverse proportion to the size of the place that produces it.' I realise that there would be many exceptions to this principle, but certainly it would be true of Chablis and its wines.

That such a small unprepossessing town, with vineyards of only limited size, should have such a worldwide reputation is truly surprising. I am certain that there is much more Californian, and New York, Chablis sold in the United States in a week than there is true Chablis produced in a year. In many countries Chablis has now become a generic term for dry white wine, or one would have thought so if it had not been for the fact that one of the top selling rosé wines in the United States also travels under label of Chablis. Many producers are now realising that it can only be short-sighted practice to continue using the term for non-genuine wines and both the French and Common Market governments have pursued its protection diligently. Nevertheless its use continues. Only recently, I saw in a German magazine Mendoza Chablis, from Argentina, being offered to the readers.

Until the coming of the A6 autoroute, the town of Chablis was largely ignored by visitors. Even the merchants of Beaune and Nuits Saint Georges, who were probably responsible for purchasing three-quarters of the total crop, rarely ventured there, relying on the brokers to bring them samples when needed. With the Chablis region little more than an hour away by road from Beaune and perhaps an hour and a half from Paris, visitors are now more numerous,

51

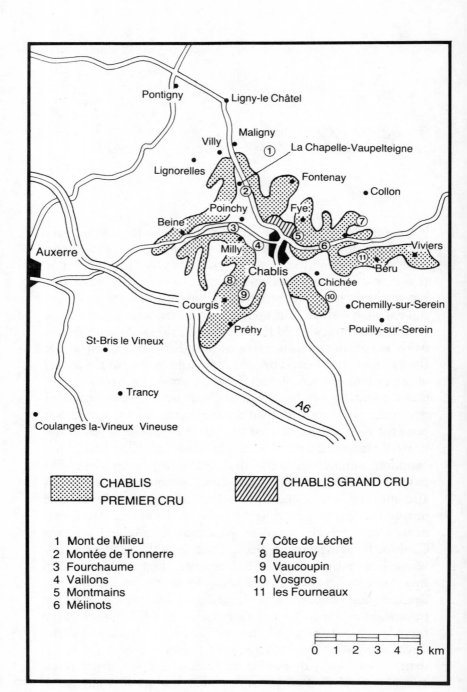

CHABLIS
PREMIER CRU

CHABLIS GRAND CRU

1 Mont de Milieu
2 Montée de Tonnerre
3 Fourchaume
4 Vaillons
5 Montmains
6 Mélinots

7 Côte de Léchet
8 Beauroy
9 Vaucoupin
10 Vosgros
11 les Fourneaux

0 1 2 3 4 5 km

though the town of Chablis itself has retained its appearance of a country backwater. Outside investment has meant that the area is now much less dominated by a host of small growers, but rather by a small number of major companies, who also offer a broad range of wines, not just from the Yonne *département* itself, but, in some cases, from throughout France.

Up to the time of phylloxera, the production of wines from the Yonne dominated that of all Burgundy. André Jullien, in *Topographie de Tous les Vignobles Connus*, whose second edition appeared in 1822, gave the production figures for the Yonne as being 900,000 hectolitres per year, as compared with the other three *départements* now producing Burgundies, namely Côte d'Or 550,000 p.a., Saône et Loire 800,000 p.a. and Rhône 560,000 p.a. In the late 1960s, before the recent expansion of the vineyard area, the comparative figures were Yonne: 115,353 hls p.a., Côte d'Or: 328,500 hls p.a., Saône et Loire: 563,175 hls p.a. and Rhône: 922, 176 hls p.a. Thus it can be seen the importance of the vineyards of the Yonne declined dramatically, during a comparatively short period of time.

As in much of Burgundy, the vineyards of the Yonne owe much of their early development to the church and more particularly the Cistercian order of monks. After the mother abbey was established at Citeaux in 1098, one of the founding monks, the Englishman Stephen Harding, went on to establish a daughter house at Pontigny, just north of Chablis, in the year 1114. It became one of the most important Cistercian monasteries, with its Abbot an ex-officio member of the General Council of the Order of Cistercians. Pontigny, in its own right carried out missionary work and had, at its peak, 45 daughter houses in Burgundy, France, Italy, Poland and England. Its connection with England was particularly strong as it became a place of refuge for those archbishops who fell out with the court. These included Thomas à Becket, Stephen Langton and Edmund of Abingdon, who was later to be canonised as Saint Edmé.

One clerical visitor to the area was Brother Salimbene, a Franciscan friar from Italy in the middle of the thirteenth century who seems to have been something of a gourmet. He praises highly the white wines of the region of Auxerre, though he considers the reds not to be the equal of those of his home country. The wines cause him to quote Solomon and say, 'Give strong drink to them that are sad, and wine to them that are grieved in mind: let them drink and forget their want, and remember their sorrow no more'. He also remembers rather wistfully an Easter meal when 'a certain Countess gave us for dinner (or rather gave to her whole court) twelve courses or diversities of food – and if the Count, her husband, had been there, then still greater plenty would have been served.'

By the middle of the sixteenth century, the wines of the area were in high demand in Paris, largely because of the ease of their delivery to the capital, as they could be shipped down the Serein and the Yonne to the Seine and the capital. In those days river transport was the fastest and the cheapest. At the Porte Saint Bernard a market was established for dealing in the wines of Auxerre and there used to be regularly as many as 170 merchants in attendance. In the anonymous *Délices de la Campagne*, which appeared in 1654, the writer says, 'The most agreeable wines by far come from Burgundy and particularly from the neighbourhood of Chably.'

That the wines of the region are considered to be Burgundies at all is a result of history. They formed part of the lands of the Dukes of Burgundy rather than of the Counts of Champagne. Indeed vineyards having the right to produce Champagne are little more than 20 miles from Chablis, whilst the main vineyards of Burgundy are 70 miles or so away.

The end of the nineteenth century proved to be disastrous for the Yonne region and its wines. Over the years certain traditions had grown up as to the rotation of crops on vineyard land. As Dr Jules Guyot said in his report to the French Minister of Agriculture in 1866, 'The vine is pulled up when twenty-five years old, and then there is an interval of ten, fifteen, twenty or thirty years before it is replanted. Apart from the exaggeration of the length of this interval, for which I feel the maximum could be five or ten years, nothing is more essential than the adoption of this method by all the *grands crus* to guarantee their continuation and profitable fruitfulness.' This extended period during which the vineyards lie fallow laid the growers open to damage at the hands of severe frosts; a regular danger in the northerly exposed vineyards of Chablis. More fallow land meant small productive holdings and a higher consequent chance of the total destruction of them. In addition, the arrival of phylloxera in 1887, some nine years after it had first been discovered on the Côte d'Or at Meursault, led to devastation of the vineyards. Two other social developments also led to the collapse of the wine trade in the Yonne. The establishment of the PLM railway line through to Lyons and the Midi opened up the Parisian markets to the vastly cheaper wines of the deep south. The speed and low cost of rail freight destroyed almost overnight the viability of many of the marginal vineyards that traditionally supplied the capital. Finally there was the industrial revolution. This came as a godsend to many of the growers who found it no longer possible to create a viable existence for themselves from making wine. They abandoned the land to make a more secure living in the industrial and commercial Paris so fully described by Zola.

To say that Chablis slept for 70 years or more may be an exaggeration, but it is not too far from the truth. Manpower was at a premium and Albert Pic, writing in the 1930s, complains that because of this shortage it was very difficult to find workers prepared conscientiously to look after the vines. From the middle of the 1950s there began a steady increase in production, due to replanting and improved treatments in the vineyards and since the beginning of the 1970s this increase has accelerated rapidly as a result of spiralling demand for the wine. It is interesting to look at comparative production figures for the various Chablis appellations since 1943:

1943–1947	11,591 hls p.a. average
1948–1952	13,101 hls
1953–1957	10,747 hls
1958–1962	16,735 hls
1963–1967	27,102 hls
1968–1972	37,649 hls
1973–1977	57,530 hls
1978–1982	81,150 hls
1983–1985	118,794 hls average

Another question is involved in the increase in production which has excited the local growers over many generations. That is, 'Exactly which vineyards should have the right to call the wines that they produce, Chablis?' This is by no means a recent question. As in many other parts of Burgundy, many names were rather more generic than specifically attached to a particular village. Thus the name of Beaune was applied to most of the red wines produced from the Côte de Beaune – unless they came from one of the villages with an equal reputation such as Volnay, Pommard or Aloxe. So it was in Chablis. As Cyrus Redding wrote in the middle of the last century, 'of the white wines of the Yonne, the best wine is produced from the *pineau blanc* alone. The chief of these is Chablis ... The second class of white wines is produced from the white *pineau* grape and the species called *plant vert*. It is made at Chablis, and in other parts of the *arrondissement*. All these wines are called Chablis, by the merchant, though of ever so inferior a quality.' As on the Côte d'Or, those growers from the village with the abused name banded together to try to protect their interests. The first moves came in 1900, when 79 growers produced a register of those vineyards that they felt should be entitled to the name Chablis, and as a further guarantee, they sealed the bungs of their barrels before shipment with an individual wax seal. This group had no legal standing and was succeeded eight years later by the similarly unofficial *Union des Propriétaires-Vignerons de Chablis*.

The first *appellation controlée* in Chablis was introduced in 1919, when a number of vineyards were specified as *grands crus*. Those from Chablis itself, and all or part of nine adjoining villages, could be called Chablis when made from the Chardonnay grape, and Petit Chablis, if made from anything else. This decree led to a number of law-suits and a judgement of December 1920 spoke specifically of kimmeridgian marl as being the soil that produced wines that could be called Chablis.

It is this soil that has been at the root of many of the subsequent controversies as to what might, and what might not, be called Chablis. In recent years there have been two opposing schools of thought on the question as to which vineyards ought to be able to produce wine under the name of Chablis. On the one side are the traditionalists, led by local grower William Fèvre. They think that only kimmeridgian soils should be permitted. Naturally most of the members of this group have vineyards on such soil and are happy that the price of Chablis should be maintained by restricted production. Opposed to them are the expansionists led by Jean Durup and Michel Laroche, whose vineyards are largely in the surrounding villages, rather than Chablis itself. They felt that other factors, such as microclimates, should be brought into consideration.

In the event, it is the expansionists who have won the day and the government officials have considerably exended the area that is allowed to produce Chablis and Chablis Premier Cru.

At the top of the quality tree of the wines from Chablis come the seven Grand Cru vineyards, which cover just over 100 hectares on a single hillside overlooking Chablis itself. These seven, and their areas under production, are:

	hectares
Les Clos	26.0475
Vaudésir	14.7136
Valmur	13.1959
Blanchot	12.7153
Preuses	11.4426
Grenouilles	9.3775
Bougros	12.6277
total	100.1201 hectares

One also comes across a wine called Chablis Moutonne Grand Cru. Whilst this is not itself a separate vineyard, its history is quite interesting. Here it is described by Albert Pic,

> The property of 128 acres called 'La Moutonne' is situated at the entrance to the valley of Vaudésir; this vineyard formerly belonged to the monks of the Abbey of Pontigny; it was bought in 1891, at the sale of national properties, by a middleman, who passed it on some weeks after the sale to a local man from Chablis, Simon Depaquit, who formerly had been a monk at Pontigny; on the deed of sale the property is described as follows; 'a vineyard of 128 acres, a portion of Vaudésir, called la Moutonne', without any explanation as to the origin of the name. The current owner now uses this name of Moutonne as a registered trade mark.

In fact this is no longer the case: the house of Long-Depaquit, the successors of Simon Depaquit, was taken over in 1967 by two Beaune companies, Albert Bichot and Joseph Drouhin. The wine which is now sold as Moutonne comes from a portion of not just the Vaudésir vineyard, but also of Preuses, totalling 2.35 hectares and has received official recognition from the French government for its slightly ambiguous status.

Whilst the position of the *grands crus* has now been long established, that of the *premiers crus* seems to be more flexible. Ten years ago, there appeared to be something under 30 vineyards within this classification. Now the figure is 40. These come in all shapes and sizes; six of them are more than thirty hectares in extent, three are less than one hectare. To make things even more complicated, permission has been given for some vineyards to adopt the name of a more famous neighbour. Thus a grower with vines in Les Lys can call his wine Chablis les Lys, Chablis Vaillons or just Chablis Premier Cru. One can see the potential advantage for the consumer, in that he should have fewer names to remember and for the producer in that he can instantly gain a better-known name for his wine and, indeed, blend a number of wines together to sell under one label, but one gains the impression that he is practising just that which he has fought against for so long, the adulteration of a reputation.

Here is a list of the forty *premier cru* vineyards, with, in brackets, the alternative name now permitted:

	hectares		
Mont de Milieu	34.8897		
Montée de Tonnerre	5.2351		
Chapelot	20.0033	(Montée de Tonnerre)	
Pied d'Aloue	6.6874	(Montée de Tonnerre)	
Côte de Bréchain	9.2790	(Montée de Tonnerre)	41.2048
Fourchaume	32.8255		
Vaupulent	8.8421	(Fourchaume)	
Côte de Fontenay	10.0460	(Fourchaume)	
l'Homme Mort	41.3732	(Fourchaume)	
Vaulorent	16.5493	(Fourchaume)	76.8106
Vaillons	14.8154		
Châtains	14.0062	(Vaillons)	
Sêcher	10.1283	(Vaillons)	
Beugnons	11.7944	(Vaillons)	
Les Lys	12.2359	(Vaillons)	
Melinots	9.8996	(Vaillons)	
Roncières	19.6001	(Vaillons)	
Les Épinottes	22.3891	(Vaillons)	114.8690
Montmains	36.3560		
Forêt	20.9486	(Montmains)	
Butteaux	40.8097	(Montmains)	98.1143
Côte de Léchet	36.4645		
Beauroy	5.8943		
Troesmes	16.8603	(Beauroy)	
Côte de Savant	21.1846	(Beauroy)	43.9392
Vau Ligneau	20.0654		
Vau de Vey	30.2586		
Vaux Ragons	12.8206	(Vau de Vey)	43.0792
Vaucoupin	26.5768		
Vosgros	6.8838		
Vaugiraut	2.4824	(Vosgros)	9.3662
Les Fourneaux	2.1325		
Morein	5.3893	(Les Fourneaux)	
Côte des Près Girots	5.9770	(Les Fourneaux)	13.4988
Côte de Vaubarousse	1.9400		
Berdiot	0.8528		
Chaume de Talvat	0.3500	(now included in the following	
Les Landes et Verjuts	5.8549	vineyard)	
Les Beauregards	0.2090		
Côte de Cuissy	9.3522	(Les Beauregards)	9.5612
TOTAL	**610.2629 hectares**		

It is not difficult to see how some of the old names have become swamped by more recent plantings.

Apart from the question of the soil that goes to make Chablis, there are other questions that have been debated long and loud in the region. Of these perhaps that which has roused the most feeling is that of the fermentation and ageing of Chablis. Traditionally, this has always done in the cask of Chablis, the *feuillette* of 132 litres. Modern thinking, well supported by both financial pressures and limitations on space, suggests that both the fermentation and the ageing should take place in vat. Few growers in Chablis use casks now for anything less than their best wines, probably just of *grand cru* quality, and many hold even these in vats. At a halfway stage is a grower like Robert Vocoret, who uses large oak *foudres* for his wines.

Over the past few years, I feel that there has been a distinct change in the style of Chablis. Not too long ago every wine lecturer used to describe the wine as having a greenish tinge and a mouth-puckering acidity. Such a wine is almost a rarity nowadays and I can remember my agreeable surprise recently when opening a bottle from the Dauvissat domain and finding just these characteristics. Perhaps modern tastes are unhappy with acidity; perhaps they prefer something blander and easier, like many of the wines of the Mâconnais. Nevertheless it seems a pity that Chablis should forfeit its distinctive character. Sales are booming in a way that suggest that the name means more than the style of the wine.

The extension of the vineyard area in Chablis and the lessening in the use of casks for ageing of the wine have both helped in the popularisation of the wine and have meant that it sells at a lower price than otherwise might have. What has happened in Chablis is typical of what has happened in many other parts of the wine-making world. It is easy to remain dogmatic and say that all the traditions should be maintained. I personally would like to see more oak used in Chablis, for I am convinced that one has better wine as a result. I am less sure that I am prepared to pay the price that might be demanded. Similarly, I am unhappy about the way in which the expansion of the area under wines has taken place; if necessary natural features have been removed at the whim of the financiers. I cannot say, however, that the wines are worse for it; I can only say that they are different. To my mind Chablis may still make good wines, sometimes even great wines, but they have lost their personality. Now Chablis is too often what one might call a 'global Chardonnay', a passepartout wine that finds instant acceptance anywhere in the world. This is probably what the consumer wants; an ever-safe wine about which he does not have to ask questions.

Whose names should one look for in Chablis? For many years the trade was dominated by the merchants of Beaune and a considerable proportion of sales are still under labels of companies outside the Chablis region. Two Beaune companies have made considerable investments in the area, as has already been mentioned. Apart from its holding in the Domaine de la Moutonne, Maison Joseph Drouhin has built up a substantial holding with parcels of vines throughout the classifications. The wines are vinified and aged at their premises in Beaune. Albert Bichot, on the other hand, have left a great deal of autonomy to their properties in Chablis under the Long-Depaquit name. Another outsider, who has raided the neighbourhood, is Patrick Ladoucette, the owner of Château de Nozet, on the Loire. For some years he has sold a premium Chablis, but his efforts to buy vineyards in Chablis were rebuffed by the local authorities. Recently, however, he purchased the company of A. Régnard et Fils, which has long sold wine not just under its own name, but also that of Albert Pic.

For many years the local trade was dominated by the local co-operative cellar, la Chablisienne. This used to account for about 40 per cent of the total production of the region, but this has now fallen to something under a third. As well as selling vast quantities of wine in bulk, the cellar has developed the astute policy of selling, as domain bottled, wines under the labels of its members — and there are more than 200 of these. As these include such surnames as Dauvissat, Laroche, Moreau and Fèvre (names perhaps more familiar as growers and merchants unconnected with the

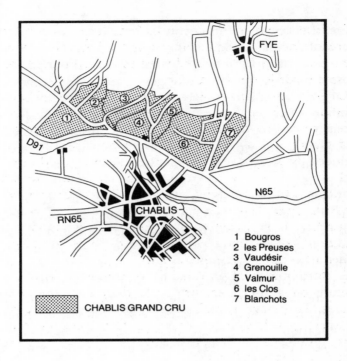

1 Bougros
2 les Preuses
3 Vaudésir
4 Grenouille
5 Valmur
6 les Clos
7 Blanchots

CHABLIS GRAND CRU

co-operative cellars), the buyer must be very careful as to what he purchases. There is no guarantee — in fact, little likelihood — that the wine in the bottle will have come from the actual producer on the label. This does not mean that it might be any less good, but the concept does leave a certain bad taste in the mouth. I must admit, it took me some time to appreciate the full implications of this means of doing business. For those keen on knowing exactly what does come from the co-operative cellar, I would suggest direct contact with them, or a look in Rosemary George's *The Wines of Chablis*, where a full list of the members is given.

Of the merchants of Chablis, the two largest are not only backed up by large domains but also have developed into selling wines, particularly white wines, from other parts of France. The company of Moreau has a domain of 70 hectares and I have particularly appreciated their Les Clos, *grand cru*, and Vaillons, *premier cru*. Whilst the vineyards still belong totally to the Moreau family, Allied Lyons, through the

Canadian company Hiram Walker, have a substantial shareholding in the merchant's business. From their domain, their most highly appreciated wine comes from the Clos des Hospices portion of Les Clos.

Of great importance too is the company of Henri Laroche, behind which is the dynamic Michel Laroche and the extensive family vineyard holdings well placed in the *grands* and *premiers crus*. Rapid expansion by this company has included the purchase of the Château de Puligny-Montrachet and some of the vineyard holdings of André Ropiteau. Particular efforts are being made to promote their wines on the British and American markets. This company, more than any other, is prepared to use both the most modern and traditional of techniques. However its wines are disguised under a host of names and labels.

A third merchant in Chablis is Simonnet-Fèbvre, who operate on a much smaller scale than the two previous houses. They have a small domain and are also noteworthy for their sparkling wines, of which they were for long the only producers. Of their Chablis, the house is perhaps proudest of its Les Preuses.

There are a host of growers in Chablis of varying reputations, but those which have not been mentioned, whose wines I have enjoyed over the years, include: Rene Dauvissat, Paul Droin, William Fèvre (Domaine de la Maladière), François Raveneau, Philippe Testut, Robert Vocoret, Alain Geoffroy, Jean Durup (Domaine de l'Eglantier and Lamblin et Fils (who are also merchants).

Outside the immediate area of Chablis, a number of other white wines are made. Of these, perhaps the most important is Petit Chablis. In past times this was produced from the Chardonnay grape in those areas not on kimmeridgian soil. As many of these have now been integrated into the appellation Chablis, the area is now smaller than it was ten years ago. Moreover yields have also tended to be lower than elsewhere, so Petit Chablis has always been a comparatively rare wine. Sadly, when the other wines in the region have been expensive, some merchants have sought to introduce the cheaper wine, thus creating an artificial demand, and once again inflating the price.

Petit Chablis should have the characteristics of a Chablis, but to a less pronounced extent. It is a wine that should be drunk young, often in the first year after its vintage, before it loses its fresh crispness. As Bernard Ginestet has said, 'Petit Chablis has no other pretention than to be a friendly wine to be drunk in its youth.'

Burgundy's second white grape, the Aligoté, is also planted quite widely in the Yonne and some growers make a speciality of it. Lamblin et Fils is one label to look out for. The village most renowned for the quality of its Aligotés is Saint Bris le Vineux, where it is almost treated as a special grape, being planted in some of the most favourite sites.

By an historical quirk this village is also renowned for a wine which has created for itself quite a cult following in Britain; this is the VDQS Sauvignon de Saint Bris. Whilst the Sauvignon grape has been officially recognised in the region since 1860 and was planted more widely in the early 1950s, there are now only 54 hectares of vineyards planted with this variety — and the figure is falling. One of the main reasons for this again lies within the village of Saint Bris. Some 15 years ago a group of local growers purchased a local quarry and started ageing *méthode champenoise* sparkling wine in its galleries. This is made with the appellation Crémant de Bourgogne, for which Sauvignon grapes may not be used. On the other hand the Aligotés of Saint Bris and the neighbouring village of Chitry are ideal, as is the historical local white, acid grape the Sacy. Growers therefore prefer to plant those grapes which can be used for making more than one type of saleable wine, rather than make a Sauvignon, whose yield is small, and which is unable to command the higher prices of its noble cousins at Sancerre, on the Loire, not too many miles away.

What is the appeal of a Sauvignon de Saint Bris? Its main attraction must be its novelty — a Sauvignon from Burgundy. In taste it resembles a Sancerre, but is a feeble imitation. For the lover of Sauvignon, there are many better wines, at lower prices coming out of Bordeaux. Sauvignon de Saint Bris is an anachronism, but a charming one.

As was said at the beginning of this chapter, the Yonne *département* used to be widely covered with vineyards. Many of these were not replanted after phylloxera, but even in lesser areas local farmers are making efforts to reintroduce the vine. At Joigny, where there was an important vineyard of more than 500 hectares during the last century, three growers are now making wine, but just from the Pinot Noir and the Pinot Gris. Similarly, at Épineuil, near Tonnerre, recent plantings have only been for the making of red wine. However one of Burgundy's vineyards with the greatest historical reputation, the three-hectare Clos de la Chainette, at Auxerre, is now planted half in Chardonnay and making *appellation controlée* wines with a recognisable quality. The property belongs to the local departmental psychiatric hospital, with the patients tending the vines. The quality must have improved, or at least the market for the wine, for it is not too long ago that an inspector reported, 'Rather than be obliged to sell the wines at a price that did not correspond to their quality, the managers of the asylum have taken the decision that they should be drunk on the spot by the inmates.'

In the nearby village of Vaux, Antoine Donat is also making award-winning wines from the Pinot and Chardonnay.

The town of Vézelay, now a scene of gastronomic as well as religious pilgrimage, has made a positive effort to recreate a reputation for its wines. In 1979 the first wine was made for almost a century, from Melon de Bourgogne and Pinot Auxerrois grapes. Chardonnay has since been planted. The appellation Bourgogne has not yet been granted, but this is expected in the near future.

Whilst it might be easy for the growers of Chablis to extend their vineyards, it is less so for those areas that have lost their renown. Science has overcome many of the problems that led to the abandonment of the vineyards of the Yonne; phylloxera has been combated and techniques have been developed to fight frost. Nevertheless, one can only admire those who are determined to plant vines in less than ideal circumstances — and with no guaranteed outlet for their produce.

6
Meursault

Strangely enough, one of the first books specifically about the wines of Burgundy was first published in London in 1728. This was written by a young tutor in Latin and French, who thought that the English ought to have more knowledge of the wines of the region of his birth. Claude Arnoux' book must have met with some success, for it was translated and integrated in full in Philip Miller's *Gardener's Dictionary*, which was one of the best-sellers of the first half of the eighteenth century.

Whilst Arnoux was born in Beaune, he seems to have had a detailed knowledge of the styles of the wines of not just the famous vineyards and villages, but also of many of the lesser ones, such as Auxey and Pernand. For Meursault, he had a great deal of admiration,

> Mulsant is, after Beaune and Nuis, the largest vineyard of Burgundy in extent; its wines are generally approved in Germany and the Low Countries, and throughout all France; I do not know whether they are so in England or not. The wines which this soil produces, in all hot and dry years, are delicious, sparkling, agreeable, warm, and beneficial; they are not dear; and if they were well chosen, they would be an honour to England, and pleasure to those that drank them. When they are kept above a year and half, they sometimes grow yellow and eager.

Meursault is a village that even in historical times enjoyed as great a reputation for its red wines as for its whites. In the

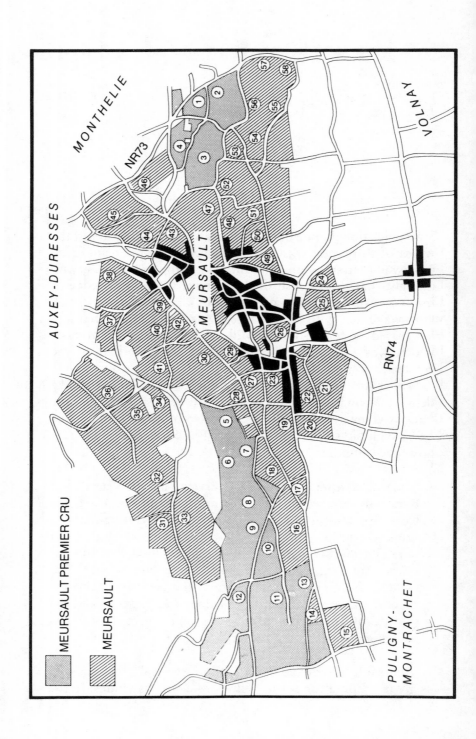

MONTHELIE

VOLNAY

NR73

AUXEY-DURESSES

MEURSAULT

RN74

PULIGNY-
MONTRACHET

MEURSAULT PREMIER CRU

MEURSAULT

MEURSAULT VINEYARDS

PREMIER CRU
1 Les Santenots Blancs
2 Les Santenots du Milieu
3 Les Plures
4 Les Cras
5 Les Gouttes d'Or
6 Les Bouchères
7 Le Porusot
8 Le Porusot Dessus
9 Les Genevrières Dessus
10 Genevrières Dessous
11 Les Charmes-Dessus
12 Les Perrières Dessous
13 Les Charmes-Dessous

MEURSAULT
14 Les Gruyaches
15 Les Pellans
16 Le Limozin
17 Le Buisson Certaut
18 Les Crotots
19 Les Pelles-Dessous
20 Les Millerands
21 Sous la Velle
22 Au Village
23 Les Meix Gagnes
24 Les Magny
25 En L'Ormeau
26 Au Village
27 Clos de Mazeray
28 En Luraule

29 Au Moulin Landin
30 Les Grands Charrons
31 Les Gorges de Narvaux
32 Les Tillets
33 Les Narvaux-Dessous
34 Les Casse-Têtes
35 Les Clous Dessous
36 Les Vireuils Dessous
37 Les Luchets
38 Les Meix Chavaux
39 Les Chevalières
40 Les Rougeots
41 Le Tesson
42 Les Petits Charrons
43 Les Meix Tavaux
44 Les Forges
45 Au Murger de Monthèlie
46 Le Pré de Manche
47 le Cromin
48 Barre Dessus
49 Clos de la Barre
50 En la Barre
51 Les Perchots
52 Les Corbins
53 Les Peutes Vignes
54 Les Criots
55 Les Vignes Blanches
56 En Marcausse
57 Les Santenots Dessous
58 En Gargouillots

nineteenth century its finest reds, which now go under the label of Volnay Santenots, were preferred by certain experts to the wines of Corton and considered to be the best of the Côte de Beaune. Also the village had highly recognised passetousgrain (wines made from a mixture of Pinot grapes at the time of pressing), that were recommended by Jullien as 'solid, very full-bodied and suitable for building up weak wines'. Camille Rodier also speaks of the passetousgrains, both white and red; the only time that I have heard of the expression used for white wines. I imagine that it must have been a wine made from a mixture of the Chardonnay and Aligoté grapes. Under current legislation, such a wine could only be sold as Bourgogne Aligoté.

Whether the name Meursault comes from the Latin words meaning 'rat jump' as Courtepée suggests, 'rat wood' as Gandelot suggests, or 'high wall' as Pierre Forgeot more logically proposes, I have no idea, but its wine history is a long one. Indeed, Forgeot suggests that the first vineyards in Burgundy were planted on the hills behind the village before the Roman invasion of Gaul. Traces have been found of a Roman villa and of two small camps, and it does have a certain strategic importance on what has been a trade route since pre-Roman times.

One of the earliest vineyards given to the Cistercian order was that in Meursault of Sybille, the daughter of Hugues of Burgundy in 1185. The same order extended its holdings there with another gift 20 years later and in 1218 it received even more from the Abbey of Tart-le-Bas, which ceded to them its vines in the village, including part of the Santenots vineyard. The château was built during the early part of the fourteenth century and the owners soon built up important vineyard holdings in the village. In 1669 half of these, together with other vines in Demoisy and Travoisy, as well as several buildings, 16 hectares of meadows and 40 hectares of other land, were left to the Hospices de Beaune by the owner Jehan de Massol, a King's Councillor in the Burgundy Parliament. The will was hotly disputed by the family but the Hospices finally benefited to what was then valued at 200,000 *livres*. Their holdings in Meursault were further increased by the decision of the Bishop of Autun in 1766, that the hospital in Meursault should be annexed to that of Beaune. Amongst the property that it brought with it were 41 *ouvrées* of vines (about 1.7 hectares in Napoleonic measurement).

Over the years the Hospices de Beaune have steadily built up their white wine vineyard holdings in Meursault and they now own something over five and a half hectares of vines there, with portions in many of the best plots including Genevrières, Charmes and Poruzot. In the 1986 vintage, for example, of the 100 hogsheads of white wine offered for auction by the Hospices, 94 came from Meursault. In all, seven *cuvées* are made from Meursault wines.

Deeds mention many of the finest vineyards of Meursault by name as early as the middle of the seventeenth century and they must have each built up their individual reputation, for we find Thomas Jefferson, in 1789, instructing the Beaune cooper Parent, who acted as his buying agent on the spot, to send him some of Monsieur Bachey's Meursault Goutte d'Or of the 1784, as it was the wine he preferred above all else. The anonymous author of a guide to the Côte d'Or, which appeared in 1818, recommends the Perrières, the Genevrières and the Goutte d'Or for their white wines, and the Santenots for its reds.

At almost the same time, Jullien praised the white wines highly, and gave some insight as to trade practices at the time.

Meursault supplies many highly rated white wines, which, when they leave the neighbourhood, often taken the name of Montrachet, which they resemble a little, but of which they are not the same quality. The slope called Perrière is particularly renowned for the excellence of its wines, which stand up to being compared with Bâtard-Montrachet; they have much finesse, delicacy and perfume. The vines called Combette, Goutte d'Or, Genevrière and Charmes, furnish wines of the same style, and which, for their merit should be classed after those of Perrière, in the order that I gave in naming them.

Auguste Luchet, who wrote a work on the wines of Burgundy of the 1857 vintage, says that the wines of Meursault are the finest white Burgundies after le Montrachet and singles out the same vineyards as Jullien, with the addition of Bouchères, Tessons and Rougeot. The one vineyard that modern raters of the finest wines of Meursault might include is les Poruzots, which seems to have been ignored by the earlier writers.

The question of ageing wine in oak is one that has already been lightly touched on in the chapter on Chablis. In my view, wines made from the Chardonnay grape positively benefit from ageing in oak, and the more full-bodied wines from new oak. It is interesting to note that the coopers of Burgundy now appear to be supplying more casks to the producers of the United States and Australia than to local growers. More questionable are the merits of actually carrying out the fermentation of white wines in cask. Stricter controls on temperature are feasible when the wine is fermented in bulk in a stainless steel vat.

Whatever one might say about the merits or otherwise of maturing white wines in cask, one dominant factor is the cost. A new oak Burgundian hogshead now costs about £300. For too many growers it is an investment they are not prepared to take. Furthermore, casks take up a lot of space and are difficult to handle. If one can obtain the same price for one's wine without ageing it in cask, why bother? Fortunately for the consumer there are still many growers who do bother. For a great white wine from the Côte d'Or, I feel that ageing in cask is obligatory; for the better wines from the Chalonnais, the Mâconnais and Chablis, it is a positive aid. Sadly, whilst the growers in those areas might agree with me, fewer and fewer of them are following their thoughts. On the other hand, for a wine like an Aligoté, which is designed to be drunk young, an oak cask will not help in the creation of the final picture that is desired.

For me the wines of Meursault have a rich nuttiness, which is often enhanced by the use of new oak casks. Of all the white wines of Burgundy, these are perhaps the ones which benefit the most from oak. For many, this is an acquired taste, but the depth of most wines of the village is able to support and gain from this positive taste. Meursault, though, supports a broad range of style of wines. Those from the Perrières, for example, which adjoin the vineyards of Puligny-Montrachet, tend, as has already been suggested, to have a great deal of finesse and delicacy, which can be overpowered by more than just a hint of oak. Such wines as the Poruzots and the Goutte d'Or, where the soil is richer and the wine more corpulent, appreciate the extra wrapping of a new cask.

Meursault is one of the very few villages of the Côte d'Or where one can get lost: it is a maze of narrow streets, peppered with signs of growers' cellars. The main square is easy to miss. On one side is the town hall, which incorporates the little that is left from the demolition of the château, after a revolt by the Burgundians against Louis XIII in 1633. Whilst this is the real château *at* Meursault, there is also the imposing Château *de* Meursault. This is built over fifteenth-century cellars constructed, like so many others, by the monks of Citeaux, and once belonged to the Comte de Moucheron. He fell on hard times and began to sell his vines and then the park in front of the château as individual building lots. I went to look at them myself, but was warned off as I was told, perhaps falsely, that there were too many mosquitoes in the summer. Two houses were built and a third was under construction, when the château itself came up for sale. It was rumoured that the British brewers Bass were about to pounce. French, or more probably Burgundian, pride was at stake and the property was bought by André Boisseaux, of Patriarche Père et Fils. He repurchased the newly constructed villas in front of the château, destroyed them and planted the park with vines, which now produce an excellent white wine. The cellars are now open for tasting a range of wines from the domain, which includes some fine wines from Beaune as well as Meursault. The profits from these tastings go to charity. The rest of the château is an art gallery.

Of more historical interest is the church of Meursault, which was built in the fifteenth century by the monks of

Cluny. Its spire, which is almost 60 metres tall, is built from local stone and is by far the highest in the region. Rather less well maintained is the Hôpital de Meursault, which lies on the main road away from the village. This was built in 1180 as a lazar-house, by Hugues of Burgundy. The importance of its financial backing can be gauged by a visit to the cellars of Ropiteau Frère et Fils in the centre of the village, for it was here that the wines made from the Hospital's vineyards used to be lodged.

Meursault's *Syndicat Viticole* lists well over 100 growers living in the village, as well as many from elsewhere, incuding the rather cryptic entry MOORE, Maguy (Heritière DREUMONT), Ross-Cottage, Grande-Bretagne. Most of the growers are on a small scale, but some are based in elegant nineteenth-century villas. Side by side are the houses of the Comte Lafon (his domain includes a slice of le Montrachet, as well as pieces of the finest vineyards in Meursault and Volnay) and Jacques Prieur (with le Montrachet, Chambertin, Musigny, Clos de Vougeot, Chevalier-Montrachet and *premier crus* in Beaune, Volnay, Meursault and Puligny-Montrachet).

The largest single holding in Meursault itself belongs to the Ropiteau family. Their merchants' business, Ropiteau Frères, was sold to the important Chantovent wine group, which also has interests in the Minervois and in Bordeaux. They were also given the exclusivity of the wines from the family vineyards, but this contract expired with the 1985 vintage. The situation at the present is rather confused, with two organisations, the Laroche company from Chablis and the Chauvenet company from Nuits Saint Georges, both claiming, with apparent justification, that they now have the sole rights to the wines from the Ropiteau domains. Local bookmakers are offering odds on Chauvenet emerging the winners from a difficult situation. Laroche has, however, bought most of the estate of one member of the family, André Ropiteau.

The main Ropiteau domain includes parts of all the major vineyards of Meursault, as well as holdings in Clos Vougeot, Beaune, Volnay, and most especially, Monthélie. This is one domain that is not afraid to experiment with new oak, even to an extent that some wine-drinkers find excessive.

The merchant company of Ropiteau Frères is now totally separate from the family, not just in shareholding terms, but also in management. Quite naturally, they have sought to built up a particular reputation for their wines from Meursault. This was much easier when the family vineyards were behind them. I hope that they can still find the quantities of wine of the quality they need to maintain their position in the white wine market. Whilst they maintain their historic cellars in the centre of the village to store some wine, and perhaps more commercially, for tourist purposes, the company has now constructed a major bottling plant, outside the village on the main road. Like many of the other companies in Burgundy, and most particularly in Beaune, they have found that old cellars in cramped premises are not the ideal place from which to run a wine company.

Another merchant's label that one can see from Meursault is that of the Société d'Élevage et de Conditionnement de Vins Fins. This is run by a local grower, Jean Germain, whose name appears on the label, in conjunction with the English broker and vineyard owner from Nuits Saint Georges, Tim Marshall. Their speciality is fine white wines from the Côte de Beaune in a traditional style and the quality is exceptional.

Of the other growers in the village, there are several that are known for the quality of their wines. Amongst those producers renowned (or is it notorious?) for using new oak, is G. Michelot. Whilst owning important portions of Charmes and Genevrières, and a small part of Perrières, most of this grower's wines are sold as plain Meursault. I must admit that I enjoy his wines, though I do think that they need rather more than the average ageing for the new oak to achieve the correct balance. They are wines that can benefit from being drunk ten years or so after the vintage.

Against the use of new oak is the Domaine Matrot, where fermentation is carried out for the most part in stainless steel, and the wine is put into second-hand casks, before being bottled young. This gives wines with more flavour and more fruit, ready for drinking young in the French style.

The domain of Robert Ampeau et Fils includes some Puligny Combettes as well as Meursault from Charmes and Perrières and la Pièce Sous le Bois at Blagny. These growers are also prepared to experiment with new techniques and, for the most part, also make full-bodied wines which keep well.

Amongst the host of growers in the village it is difficult to select just a few other worthy of mention. The wines of Coche-Dury are renowned for their full-bodied flavour and this is due to the maker's insistence on not filtering his wines. (This is a tradition also at the Comte Lafon domain.) Over the years I have also enjoyed the Clos des Bouches Chères, the Poruzot of the René Manuel domain, which is now distributed by the Nuits Saint Georges shipper Labouré-Roi, and the wines of local grower and broker Patrick Javilier.

The village of Meursault also has an important part to play in the wine calendar of Burgundy. It is here that the third of the Trois Glorieuses takes place each November. At lunchtime, on the day after the Hospices de Beaune sale, is the Paulée de Meursault. A *paulée* is the traditional meal that is offered by a vineyard owner to his workers, when all the grapes have been brought safely in. In 1923 the then Comte Lafon invited the growers of Meursault to a paulée; also invited were a few journalists and the Baron de Granmaison, who was the Grand Master of the Sacavins d'Anjou. As the guests arrived at Meursault station at eight o'clock in the morning, the time before lunch had to be filled in by visiting a few cellars. Only 35 guests reached the table. Now, because of the limited size of the largest room in the village, only 300 can attend the Paulée — and I am certain that British fire authorities would put the maximum at about 150!

Of all the banquets in Burgundy, the Paulée must be the most relaxed. No wine is provided with the eight-course meal; you are expected to bring, and share, your own. There is a great deal of luck as to who is sharing your table as there might be on it anything from a 1929 Goutte d'Or to an 1986 Aligoté, or even a bottle of English or Californian wine. On the one occasion that I attended the Paulée, I was not well prepared. The meal is due to start at about midday. By five o'clock, we had eaten the *Terrine de Lièvre au Parfait de Foie*

Gras, La Meurette d'Anguilles au Vin de Meursault and the *Paupiettes Morvandelles*. *Le Gigot d'Agneau Façon des Moutardiers avec sa Garniture de Légumes* was on the horizon, but we had to leave to catch our plane.

I have admiration for those who manage the three banquets, on the successive days of the Hospices de Beaune weekend, but I feel sure that the growers of Meursault were laughing up their sleeves when they decided to have the Paulée as the climax. It is almost reminiscent of the eating contests described by Damon Runyon. In Mindy's Restaurant 'No talking and rooting from the spectators is permitted'. At Meursault, however, it is a much more jovial affair. There is, however, a more serious side to the Paulée. Each year a literary award is made, with the lucky winner receiving 100 bottles of Meursault.

To the south of Meursault, on the hillside below the tree-line, lies the hamlet of Blagny, whose vineyards are split between the two villages of Meursault and Puligny-Montrachet. For centuries the land had ecclesiastical overlords, first the Bishop and Chapter of Langres, who were the most important vineyard owners on the Côte d'Or after the Cistercian order, and then the Abbot of Maizières. Some time after the Revolution the chapel fell into the hands of Leonce Bocquet, who in 1889 had bought the Château at Clos Vougeot, the press-house and some fifteen hectares of vines. It was he who restored the château and occupied it some 300 years after work on it had begun. The Château de Blagny now belongs, as does the chapel, to the Comtesse de Montlivaut.

In vinous legal terms, Blagny holds a peculiar legal position. Its red wines can be sold as Blagny and its whites as Puligny-Montrachet or Puligny-Blagny or Meursault or Meursault-Blagny, depending on which side of the boundary the vineyard lies. Henri Cannard, in his *Balades en Bourgogne*, claims that the soil of Blagny is much more suited to the production of red wines than white. It is commercial considerations that have dictated that the production of the latter is now much more important. Whatever the soil may say, there is no doubt that the four vineyards on the

Meursault side of the village are capable of producing excellent white wines. Amongst recent wines that have impressed me are a Château de Blagny 1982, distributed by Louis Latour and a Sous le Dos d'Âne 1983 from Henri Clerc, whose intense fruit gave an impression of lime marmalade.

7
Puligny–Montrachet

Burgundy is full of improbabilities, but Puligny-Montrachet has one of the strangest. On the main square lies the hotel-restaurant, Le Montrachet, which has been built up over the last few years from a local village inn to a highly-rated restaurant, rosetted in Michelin. Nothing strange about that, you might feel: Burgundy is noted for its restaurants. However, this restaurant belongs to a doctor and his wife from Arras in the north of France. Apparently he went to school in England, and his proudest possession is the cap that he was awarded for cricket. He dreams of creating a cricket team in Puligny and playing a succession of touring teams from England. Sadly, since starting this chapter, I have learnt that the family have sold a majority holding in the restaurant and also their house in Puligny. I only hope that this does not mean the end of my dreams of sitting under the plane trees with a glass of Puligny in my hand watching a gentle game of cricket.

Most of the growers in the village dream rather less. A higher proportion of wine than elsewhere is domain bottled and that means that the little that is sold in cask is competed for by the *négociants*, with open cheque-books. Puligny is a wine that is much in demand, not just because it comes from a village that owns two *grand crus* in entirety, and two others in partnership, but also because it is many people's ideal white wine. In Puligny, finesse, elegance and fruit coincide. Some may prefer the rich roundness of a Meursault, but no one will deny the brilliance of the ideal Puligny.

If Puligny-Montrachet makes the finest white Burgundies, then le Montrachet is the finest of the fine. The total area of the

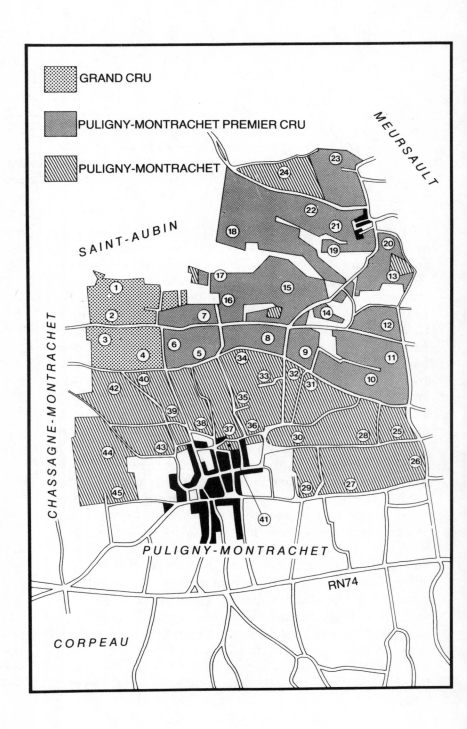

PULIGNY-MONTRACHET VINEYARDS

GRAND CRU

1 Chevalier Montrachet
2 Montrachet
3 Bâtard Montrachet
4 Bienvenues Bâtard
   Montrachet

PULIGNY-MONTRACHET
  PREMIER CRU

5 Clos des Meix
6 Les Pucelles
7 Le Cailleret
8 Clavoillons
9 Les Perrières
10 Les Referts
11 Les Combettes
12 Champ Canet
13 Les Chalumeaux
14 Clos de la Garenne
15 Ez Folatières
16 Au Chaniot
17 Peux Bois
18 Champ Gain
19 La Truffière
20 Sous le Courthil
21 Hameau de Blagny
22 La Garenne ou sur la
   Garenne

23 Sous le Puits

PULIGNY-MONTRACHET

24 Le Trézin
25 Les Charmes
26 Corvée des Vignes
27 Les Reuchaux
28 Les Levrons
29 Derrière la Velle
30 Au Paupillot
31 Les Nosroyes
32 Les Petites Nosroyes
33 Les Grands Champs
34 Brelance
35 Voitte
36 Les Boudrières
37 La Rue aux Vaches
38 Les Meix
39 Rue Rousseau
40 Les Enseignères
41 Au Village
42 Les Aubues
43 Noyer Bret
44 Les Tremblots
45 Les Houlières

vineyard is 7.998 hectares, with fractionally the larger part in Puligny-Montrachet. Here the general exposition is south-east and there are those specialists who claim that better wine comes from these vines than from the more southerly exposed vines of Chassagne. Lucky is he who has the opportunity of tasting le Montrachet; doubly lucky is he who tastes one from Puligny and one from Chassagne; foolish is he who claims to have tasted enough of them to be able to make definitive qualitative judgements about the merits of which way the vine faces.

Over the centuries, the Montrachet has had the writer turning to his thesaurus to find adjectives that give a true representation of his feelings, without repeating what others have said before. Perhaps it is worthwhile quoting what Arnoux said about it at the beginning of the eighteenth century,

Morachet is a little plot of ground between Chassagne and Puligny, in the plain, which is in possession of one vein of earth, which renders its soil wholly of the same kind; it produces a white-wine the most curious and most delicious in France; there is no wine of Côte-Rotie, Muscat, nor Frontignan that equals it. It produces but a very small quantity, and it sells very dear; and in order to have a small quantity of it, it ought to be bespoke a year before; because this wine is always bespoke before it is made. But great caution is to be taken not to be deceived, for the neighbouring vineyards of this close partake a little of the quality, and oftentimes pass for Morachet, and therefore it will be absolutely necessary to have a faithful correspondant. This wine has those qualities that neither the Latin nor the French tongue can express: I have drunk of it of six or seven years old, and am not able to express its delicacy or excellence.

Even during Victorian times, when rich sweet wines were the fashion, Montrachet seems to have held its own. Cyrus Redding said that it was the 'French Tokay, in the opinion of many connoisseurs, but only in renown, for these wines bear little resemblance to each other.' Later French writers have put it on a par with Château d'Yquem, but this is unfair to both of them. For those who like a dry white wine, one reigns supreme, for those who prefer a sweet, the other.

There have been vines on the site for many centuries. As early as 1482, François de Perrières, Lord of Chassagne, included in his inventory five ouvrées of vines in Montrachet and five years earlier a sale was made of fourteen ouvrées of vines in the spot known as Sous-le-Montrachet. According to Malte-Brun, the major owner from the sixteenth to the eighteenth century was the Clermont-Montoizon family, whose holding was bought at the time of the French Revolution by a certain Monsieur Pourtalès. In 1855, Dr Lavalle gives the names of six owners, of whom the first is the Marquis de la Guiche. Today, his successor the Marquis de Laguiche is still the major owner with two hectares, just about a quarter of the total vineyard. It is not just in these days that the wine of the Marquis de la Guiche draws the plaudits. In the last century, a certain Monsieur de Cussy may have been hoping for a few bottles as a present when he wrote, 'O Montrachet, divine Montrachet! The first, the finest of those white wines that our rich France produces. You who have remained so pure and spotless in the hands of your honourable owner, M. le Marquis de la Guiche, I salute you in admiration!' Alexis Lichine, in his *Wines of France*, which first appeared in 1952, lists twelve owners in Le Montrachet. The latest list names seventeen, who include, as well as the Marquis de Laguiche such well-known names as Baron Thénard, Bouchard Père et Fils, Jacques Prieur and the Comte Lafon. Two names that have disappeared are Roland Thévenin and the Comte de Moucheron. Both their properties were bought by the Domaine de la Romanée-Conti.

As Anthony Hanson points out, the name Montrachet on a wine label is no guarantee of value for money or even of a great wine. Even in this vineyard the wine does not make itself. All that it does is to provide the best of all possible raw materials. Of the wines that I have tasted, the best have come from the Marquis de Laguiche, whose wine is made for him by Joseph Drouhin, the Domaine de la Romanée-Conti,

Comte Lafon and Bouchard Père et Fils. It is fair to say, however, that I have no experience of the majority of the producers' Montrachet.

One important point about serving Montrachet is that it should not be served chilled, but rather at just above cellar temperature, say 14°C. It is only in this way that the magnificent aroma of the wine can be fully appreciated.

Interestingly, there must have been growing criticism of the quality of Montrachet and its fellow *grand cru* neighbours from Puligny and Chassagne, for in a decree of February 1987 the legislation for these appellations was changed. In future, Montrachet and Chevalier Montrachet must have twelve degrees of natural alcohol minimum before chaptalisation, and the others eleven and a half degrees. Previously, these minimum strengths could be obtained with chaptalisation. In addition, any of these wines which is chaptalised must not pass fourteen and a half degrees, or else it loses its right to the appellation.

As has already been mentioned, since the earliest times, passing off has been a problem with Montrachet. Indeed various terms were used over the ages to distinguish the king from his court. Thus we have Montrachet Ainé and Vrai Montrachet to separate the one from the Bâtard, the Chevalier and the others.

Above le Montrachet, where the slope gets steeper, lies the seven and a half hectare vineyard of Chevalier-Montrachet. In quality, this is considered to be the closest runner to le Montrachet. One of the reasons for this is no doubt because amongst the owners are some of the best-known merchants of Burgundies — companies that have the means to promote their wines around the world. Amongst these names are Louis Latour, Louis Jadot, Bouchard Père et Fils and domains like Jacques Prieur, Leflaive and Jean Chartron, whose wines are distributed by the recently formed house of Chartron and Trebuchet.

Chevalier-Montrachet has the reputation of being a wine with an appealing delicacy, a wine that matures comparatively early and can be drunk much younger than a Montrachet. Of outstanding note is the Chevalier-Montrachet les Demoiselles, part of the vineyard that is shared by those longstanding friends and rivals Louis Latour and Louis Jadot. By tradition, part of the Cailleret vineyard has right to the appellation Chevalier-Montrachet. The only Chevalier-Montrachet that I have tasted recently was a cask sample of the 1985 vintage from Bouchard Père et Fils, whose softness came as a surprise after the intensely deep nose.

Bâtard-Montrachet is the largest of the *grand cru* vineyards of Puligny and Chassagne, being almost twelve hectares in extent. Like le Montrachet, it is split between the two villages, with, once again, the slightly larger portion being in Puligny. The fragmentation is intense, with 46 different growers on the register. As many family names occur more than once, it is probable that some of these may be vinified together. Among the well-known names are Joseph Drouhin, the Domaine de la Romanée-Conti, Leflaive, Henri Clerc and Albert Morey.

Cyrus Redding, writing in 1860, noted the vast difference in price that the three wines of Montrachet, Chevalier-Montrachet and Bâtard-Montrachet demanded. 'These vineyards have all the same south-eastern aspect, yet the wine from them is so different in quality, that while Montrachet sells for twelve hundred francs the hectolitre, the Chevalier brings but six hundred and Bâtard only four hundred.' As a matter of comparison today, I see that a London wine merchant is offering the same three wines, from the same source, of the 1984 vintage, at the following prices per case of twelve bottles: le Montrachet, £615; Bâtard-Montrachet £405; Chevalier-Montrachet £375. This would seem to suggest, and I do not think this to be wholly true, that the reputation of Bâtard-Montrachet has increased at the expense of the Chevalier.

The vineyard of Bâtard-Montrachet lies below the lane that goes directly from Meursault to Chassagne, above the village of Puligny. The soil is rather richer than that of Chevalier-Montrachet and the wines take longer to show at their best.

The vineyard of Bienvenues-Bâtard-Montrachet is effectively part of Bâtard-Montrachet, being the south-west corner. In all it extends to 3.68 hectares and the soil and the exposition are identical to Bâtard-Montrachet. In 1977, the local growers suggested that the smaller appellation should be dropped in favour of the larger one, but there seems to have been no movement on this project since. Some fifteen growers share the appellation and amongst the better-known names, those of Leflaive, Sauzet, Carillon, Henri Clerc and Ramonet appear once more.

Apparently, in historical times, the vineyard of Bâtard-Montrachet used to belong to the Lord of Puligny and he used to let out part of it to workers who would pay him with a proportion of their crop. Such workers were known as the *bienvenues*, which is how part of the vineyard gained a separate name.

In addition to its four *grand crus*, Puligny has a number of *premier cru* vineyards with a very high reputation. The best of these are the continuation of the same slope of the *grand cru* vines, lying on approximately the same level and facing in the same direction. Immediately next to le Montrachet, though separated from it by a narrow lane, lies le Cailleret. The Clos de Cailleret is sold by Joseph Drouhin. Lying lower on the slope is les Pucelles, which is also renowned for its finesse. Here the names to look out for include Chartron et Trebuchet and the Leflaive domain. An enclave within this vineyard is the Clos des Meix, a monopoly of the Sauzet domain.

Of all the growers in the village, it is perhaps the Leflaive family who have the biggest fan club. The chairperson of this must be Serena Sutcliffe, who enthuses:

> Quite simply, this domain makes some of the best white wines in Burgundy, ergo, the whole of the world. They own no Montrachet (if it was in my gift, I would love to give them a few plots I could name, and watch the improved results!) but have a magnificent spread of the other wines. There are few things more pleasant in life than trying to decide with M. Vincent Leflaive if his Bienvenues, his Bâtard or the unbelievable Chevalier is reminiscent of hawthorn, blackthorn or mayblossom. At the last attempt,

I detected lavender honey in the Chevalier. Then there is floral Pucelles, rich Combettes, greengages on young Clavoillon and limetree blossom on the straight Puligny. There is always undeniable quality and breed.

There are few, including myself, who would disagree with the sentiments behind the judgement, though for many of us the scents of the countryside do not come quite so easily! Vincent Leflaive is not one who believes that, as far as white wines are concerned, quantity and quality are totally related. As he points out, there were no complaints about the quality of his wines of the 1982 vintage, when his yields, in certain cases, were two or three times the average.

Etienne Sauzet was, until his death in 1974, one of the most widely respected growers of Burgundy. There were different opinions about his wines, with certain experts claiming that they oxidised too soon. Whilst the Sauzet label still survives, the domain is now run by his son-in-law Gérard Boudot, whose wines are now considered amongst the best from Puligny. Monsieur Boudot is someone who thinks about his wine-making and has carried out extensive research into alternative methods. As a result, chill treatment to avoid tartar crystals is firmly rejected and the membrane method of filtration has been accepted as the one which leaves the wine with the maximum amount of fruit.

Another grower prepared to experiment is Louis Carillon. His researches have been mainly in the direction of ageing in wood. He firmly believes that ageing in new wood improves the flavour of a wine not just in the short term. In a report on a seminar held in California on the Chardonnay grape, he is quoted in the *Wine Spectator* as saying, 'Wood pulls a wine up, helps it, improves the quality and new barrels make the flavour more persistent.'

The Château of Puligny-Montrachet used to belong to the Burgundian poet and winemaker Roland Thévenin, but it has recently been purchased by the Laroche family of Chablis, as a prestigious headquarters for their expansion into the white wines of the Côte d'Or.

The church at Puligny is worth a visit. It dates back to the thirteenth century and contains a number of early wooden statues. During some excavations in the nineteenth century, a metal box was found in which was a parchment inscribed in Latin:

In the year of Our Lord 1604, on the fourth day of the moon of the month of October, We, Peter Saulnier, Bishop of Autun, have consecrated this altar in honour of the Blessed Virgin Mary, and we have buried here the relics of Saint Isidore, martyr. We grant to each of those faithful in Christ, who once visit this church, on this day, or on the anniversary of its consecration, forty days of indulgence in the accustomed form.

Puligny is a quiet, unspoilt village that is worth a visit for its wines, its restaurant, and perhaps also for its 40 days of indulgence!

Chablis — the gateway to Burgundy.

The vineyards of Chablis.

The village of Saint Bris renowned for its aligotés, its sauvignons and its sparkling wines.

Arriving at the Meursault Paulée, the third of the Trois Glorieuses, to which everyone brings their bottles.

A thirteenth-century wine-press at Laroche domain in Chablis.

Vintage time in Meursault.

Traditional vaulted Burgundian wine-cellars; those of the Prosper
Maufoux in the village of Santenay.

Le Montrachet — the best dry white wine vineyard in the world.

The village of Chardonnay in the Maconnais — which gave its name to the great white grape of Burgundy.

The village of Rully on the Côte Chalonnaise.

Pouilly-Fuissé at harvest time with the rock of Solutré in the distance.

After the vintage, the pressed grape skins, or *marc*, wait to be taken off for distillation, at the co-operative cellars of Lugny in the Maconnais.

8
Chassagne Montrachet

For me Chassagne-Montrachet is in many ways an unsatisfactory village. Its vineyards are split in two by the N6, with
the finest wines produced on the far southerly side of the
road. The village itself seems to lack any architectural
distinction, and the growers seem undecided whether their
fortune lies in making red wines, for the most part, or in
extending their plantings in Chardonnay. Whilst white wine
has been made in the village for centuries, it has more
generally been known for its red wines. As the latest booklet
of wines selected by the Chevaliers du Tastevin, Burgundy's
select drinking brotherhood says, 'Apart from the wines
produced from the celebrated white wine plots Montrachet
and Bâtard-Montrachet, Chassagne owes its immemorial
reputation to the red wines which are produced within its
boundaries.' Auguste Luchet, writing in 1858, does not
mention any of its white wines apart from its *grands crus*,
and Camille Rodier, approximately 70 years later, writes, 'If
you exclude the vineyards called Montrachet and Bâtard-
Montrachet producing white wines, you can only find a few
ouvrées, planted here and there, in Pinot Blanc.' More
recently, things have changed. In 1952 approximately 30 per
cent of the wine sold as Chassagne-Montrachet was white,
now it is something over 40.

One must assume that there has been no significant
geological change in the village in the recent past, so one
imagines that, for commercial reasons, white wines are now
being made on a number of vineyards that have been
considered historically more suitable for the production of

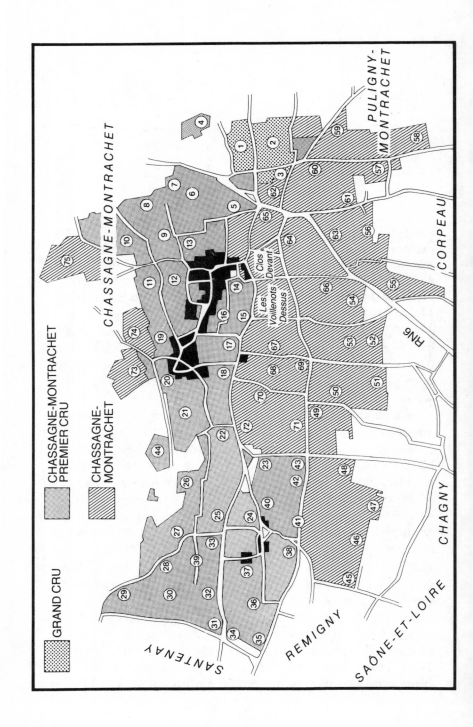

CHASSAGNE-MONTRACHET VINEYARDS

GRAND CRU
1 Le Montrachet
2 Bâtard Montrachet
3 Les Criots

CHASSAGNE-MONTRACHET
  PREMIER CRU
4 En Remilly
5 Les Bondues
6 Les Chenevottes
7 Les Pasquelles
8 Petingeret
9 Les Vergers
10 Les Chaumées
11 Clos Saint-Jean
12 Les Rebichets
13 Les Macherelles
14 Les Places
15 Ez Crets
16 Chassagne
17 La Maltroie
18 Les Champs Gain
19 Chassagne du Clos
   Saint-Jean
20 Vigne Derrières
21 En Cailleret
22 Les Fairendes
23 La Boudriotte
24 Vigne Blanche
25 Les Petits Clos
26 Les Grandes Ruchottes
27 La Romanée
28 Bois de Chassagne
29 Les Baudines
30 Les Embazées
31 Clos Pitois
32 Francemont
33 Les Grands Clos
34 La Grande Borne
35 Clos Chareau
36 Les Brussonnes

37 Morgeot
38 La Chapelle
39 Tête du Clos
40 Ez Crottes
41 Guerchère
42 Les Chaunes
43 Champs Jendreau
44 En Virondot

CHASSAGNE-MONTRACHET
45 Les Battaudes
46 Les Benoites
47 Champs de Morjot
48 La Platière
49 La Goujonne
50 Les Morichots
51 Les Lombardes
52 Le Poirier
53 Le Concis du Champs
54 Les Chambres
55 Bouchon de Corvée
56 Les Pierres
57 Fontaine Sot
58 Plante Saint Aubin
59 Les Houillères
60 Les Charrieres
61 Les Perclos
62 Blanchot Dessous
63 Dessous les Mues
64 Champ Derrière
65 La Bergerie
66 Voillenot-Dessous
67 Les Chênes
68 La Canière
69 Clos Bernot
70 Les Masures
71 Le Clos Reland
72 Les Chaumes
73 Pot Bois
74 Le Parterre
75 En Pimont

red wines. It may well be that some of these soils were of ambivalent style, for even in the complicated geological structure of the Burgundian vineyards, that of Chassagne is notoriously jumbled. Interestingly enough, at the middle of the nineteenth century, it was the village on the Côte d'Or where the most Pinot Beurot was planted.

It is noteworthy that the legislation has separate lists of vineyards with the right to *premier cru* status for the red and the white wines. In some instances, just part of a vineyard can make a *premier cru* white wine, whilst part makes a red; in others the whole vineyard makes either red or white.

Within the boundaries of Chassagne lie just under a half of the two *grand cru* vineyards, le Montrachet and Bâtard-Montrachet, but these have been discussed at length in the previous chapter. However, the village does have a monopoly of one *grand cru*; that is the Criots-Bâtard-Montrachet. With a total size of just over one and a half hectares, it is the smallest *grand cru* on the Côte d'Or, apart from La Romanée, and it is also the most southerly. It lies just to the north of the RN 6, separated from the adjacent Bâtard-Montrachet by a narrow track.

As a distinct vineyard name Criots seems to have separated itself from Bâtard-Montrachet in comparatively recent times. There is no mention of it as a distinct entity in such classic writers on Burgundy as Lavalle and Rodier. It takes its name from the Burgundian diminutive word for chalk — and this gives a good idea of the texture of the soil. Whilst the size of the vineyard may not have changed, its production has, and there are now about 550 cases made each year. This production is shared by seven growers, whose names are not widely known. Amongst the owners, one is listed with an address in Senegal and another also has, or had, a dog which bit my fellow writer on the wines of Burgundy, Anthony Hanson. The label that you are most likely to see is that of Delagrange-Bachelet, though he no longer appears on the list of owners of the local *syndicat viticole*.

In a list of the vineyards of the *arrondissement* drawn up by the local Agricultural Committee in 1861, it is interesting to note that at the top of the list under the entry for

Chassagne-Montrachet comes les Montrachets, followed by les Bâtards Montrachets; both of them in the plural. Under the entry for Puligny comes Mont-Rachet, followed by Bâtard-Montrachet, in the single. It must be assumed then that the lesser *grands crus* of the two villages were not separated as they are today.

Those vineyards that have the right to make *premier cru* white wine are: Morgeot (part), Abbaye de Morgeot (part), la Boudriotte, la Maltroie, Clos Saint Jean, les Chenevottes, les Champs-Gain, Grandes Ruchottes, la Romanée, les Brussonnes, les Vergers, les Macherelles, Chassagne (sometimes known as Cailleret). Of these Ruchottes, at least, has a reputation for making white wine going back to the last century. It is one of a group of vineyards to the south of the village, considered to make fuller-bodied wines. Also in this group are Morgeot, Cailleret, Vignes Blanches and Champs-Gain. The largest owner in Ruchottes is Ramonet-Prudhon, one of the great traditional names of Burgundy, with long-standing sales to both the United States and Great Britain. He has been criticised by some for the unevenness of the quality of his wines, but I have never had a disappointing bottle. Of the white wines from Morgeot, I think that the most enjoyable that I have tasted came from the domain of the Duc de Magenta, the descendant of the Napoleonic general MacMahon. That of the Blain-Gagnard domain can also be recommended. In Caillerets, a major grower is Delagrange-Bachelet, with about a hectare of vines — his wine is recommended by Serena Sutcliffe. A year or two ago, I can remember drinking a 1978 vintage wine from Jean-Noel Gagnard that had a long way to go.

Just to the north of the village comes another group of vineyards offering wines in a rather lighter style, with a more elegant nose and rather more finesse, approaching the style of some of the wines of Puligny. In descending order of size, these are les Chenevottes, les Chaumées, les Vergers and les Macherelles. Whilst these wines are most appealing, they are rarely seen. This may be because none of the more fashionable growers appears to have holdings there.

Of the other growers in Chassagne that have not been mentioned, one of my favourites is Albert Morey et Fils, who have a broad range of wines including Bâtard-Montrachet, Chassagne Morgeot and Caillerets and red wines from Santenay and Beaune, as well as from Chassagne. Bernard Morey, who runs this domain, is a firm believer in the value of new oak in making white wines, and is convinced that the use of a proportion each year adds finesse to the wine.

Also based in the village is the vineyard holding of the Marquis de Laguiche, whose wines are made by the Beaune company Joseph Drouhin. As well as a major slice of the Montrachet vineyard, both red and white vines are owned in Morgeot. For years, the interests of the Marquis in the village were looked after by one of those magnificent Burgundian priests, Abbé Colin, who found — or rather made — time not only to look after the spiritual life of the village, but also the temporal, as mayor, and vinous, as the arch evangelist of the merits of its wines.

Much of the village's history can be traced through the vineyard names. From prehistoric times comes the drolly named white wine Tonton Marcel, apparently after a dolmen, which has subsequently disappeared. From Roman times is la Romanée; the Abbaye de Morgeot remains as a wine and as a small chapel, belonging to the Duc de Magenta. Wine has played the dominant part in the life of the village since early times and peculiarly it appears that some white wine was made as long ago as the fourteenth century, for in the year 1383, the local lord gave instructions for the planting of the Saulvoignien grape — which is none other than the Savagnin, the grape of the *vins jaunes* of the Jura vineyards of Château-Chalon and Arbois.

If the reputation of the wines of Chassagne-Montrachet has changed over the past few years, with the increase in demand for the white wines of Burgundy, the growers have been the first to benefit. Certainly, the best white wines have attained a standing, and a price, that the reds have never had. If this has led to the consumer having a better choice, it is to the good, only as long as the wines are well made and come from those vineyards suited to the making of white wine.

There is no doubt that some of the wines that have appeared under the village name have not been worthy of the price. Certain growers have been rightly criticised by such as Serena Sutcliffe for careless wine-making. Is this any worse than in any other village on the Côte d'Or? Probably not, but the change in emphasis in the colour of the wines of Chassagne could be a Pandora's box. One must hope that it is not.

9
Other White Wines of the Côte d'Or

It is only too easy to forget that white Burgundy exists outside such fashionable names as Chablis, Mâcon, Pouilly-Fuissé, Meursault, Chassagne and Puligny. One can perhaps remember such luxuries as Corton-Charlemagne, but white wine is produced in every village appellation of the Côte de Beaune, apart from Pommard and Volnay, and also in a limited number of villages of the Côte de Nuits. Even though the sales of white Burgundies have rocketed, however, it is comparatively rare to find much change in the 'colour' of vineyards on the Côte d'Or, though it is probable that in historical times, when there was a tradition of planting a proportion of white vines in red wine vineyards, to add finesse to the wine, more white wine was made. As that indefatigible traveller and vineyard pioneer in both Australia and New Zealand, James Busby, wrote after a visit in 1831, 'They are getting rid of the white grapes in the Clos Vougeot, for the vines not only produce less, but the price of white wine never rises so high as that of the red wines. It is no uncommon thing for a hogshead of the latter to bring from 1250 to 1500 francs, but the white wine never rises above 600 francs the hogshead.' Even a century and a half ago, commercialism ruled, as it does today.

In historical times, the vineyards of the Côte d'Or came right to the gates of Dijon, but urban expansion has effectively pushed these back to Marsannay. However, the vine is striking back. For centuries the wines of les Marcs d'Or at Larrey had a fine reputation, largely as an island of Pinot Noir in a sea of Gamay. As long ago as 587 AD the Burgundian king Gontran had given the vineyard to the monks of Saint Bénigne. For some time the wine was made by the reputed company of Faiveley in Nuits Saint Georges. However the land was sold to finance the creation of the artificial lake named after Dijon's most famous mayor, Canon Kir. For more than twenty years, the name was no more than a memory, but at the beginning of 1981, a small portion of the Clos des Marcs d'Or, just 32 ares, which had not been developed, was replanted in Chardonnay by the city authorities. As the city has no resident vignerons amongst its labour force, the vineyard has been rented out for the annual sum of 450 bottles, beginning with the 1987 vintage.

On the more regular vineyard slopes of the Côte de Nuits, white wine vineyards are no more than pockets of resistance in a sea of red. Whilst Marsannay's reputation has been firmly based on its rosé wines made from the Pinot Noir grape, a little white wine is made by the Fougeray de Beauclair domain. As Marsannay now has, for the first time, an individual village appellation, this is a wine of which more might be seen in the future. One of the partners in the domain is Bernard Clair-Däu, formerly of the domain of his family name, much of which has recently been absorbed by the Beaune merchants, Louis Jadot. The next comes at the village of Fixin where Bruno Clair makes a white wine from the Pinot Blanc, rather than from the Chardonnay. Moving south, white wine is produced in the Monts-Luisants vineyard in Morey-Saint Denis. This lies at the top of the slope, where erosion over the centuries has carried away most of the soil. The Ponsot domain makes about twelve to fifteen hogsheads of a wine that to me tastes more of a white Rhône wine than a Burgundy. One critic has compared it to the white wine of Pernand-Vergelesses, and said that it should be aged for ten years before drinking. For me it has rather less interest.

As has already been mentioned, at one time Clos Vougeot used regularly to produce white wine. Now it makes none and indeed the laws forbid it. However, just in front of the entrance to the château is the Clos Blanc de Vougeot, which belongs to the Dijon company perhaps better known for the production of its cassis liqueur, l'Héritier-Guyot. The total extent of the vineyard is just over three hectares, with an average white wine production of 45 hectolitres per year. Feelings about the wine are somewhat mixed. Dr Morelot compared it to a Montrachet; Serena Sutcliffe feels that it 'lacks excitement'. On the one occasion on which I have tasted it, I tend towards the latter judgement, though, like most white wines from the Côte de Nuits, it has a rich southern taste that is foreign to Burgundy. Apparently, the monks at Clos Vougeot used to use it as their wine for mass. Perhaps, even in those days, it needed some transformation.

Behind Clos Vougeot is the *grand cru* vineyard of Musigny, one of only two *grands crus* in Burgundy producing both red and white wine (the other is Corton). Again the production is very small, and restricted to just one grower, the Comte Georges de Vogüé. From an area of 33 ares planted in Chardonnay, an average of just over four hogsheads are produced each year. Once again its resemblance to a traditional white Burgundy is minimal and there are some who claim that when tasted blind it is often mistaken for a red wine. At the price that is asked for it I feel that it is a pity to drink it blind. You need all your wits about you.

The next recognised white wine from the Côte de Nuits is again an oddity, though a well documented one. In the early 1940s Henri Gouges noticed that one of his Pinot Noir vines was producing white grapes. He took cuttings from this plant and in 1944 planted approximately half a hectare of the Nuits Saint George *premier cru* vineyard La Perrière to make white wine from this Pinot Noir clone. The wine is very full-bodied and almost blowsily opulent in style.

Of all the white wines of the Côte de Nuits, the one that I have appreciated the most is the Nuits Saint Georges Clos Arlots. Once again the production in white is minute, and there is rather more in red, but it has much more of the characteristics of a white Burgundy than its Côte de Nuits colleagues. The vineyard is squeezed between the woods on the steep hillside and the main road; it, has its own micro-climate, and a small stream, the Arlot.

As you can see, I am not much of an enthusiast for the white wines of the Côte de Nuits, as I think their rarity, and eccentricity, scarcely justify the high prices that must be asked for them. A small amount of wine is also made, in a more traditional style, with the appellation Côte de Nuits Villages. Peculiarly, whilst the Côte de Nuits is known especially for its red wines, and the Côte de Beaune for its white wines, the Villages appellation can also be used for white wines from the Côte de Nuits, but not from the Côte de Beaune.

The Côte de Nuits whimpers to an end as far as its wines are concerned, but finishes statuesquely with the marble quarries of Prémeaux, Comblanchien and Corgoloin. I recently saw these three villages described as the Côte des Pierres, which seems to be following the seaside tradition that every resort must have its Côte, be it d'Azur, Opale or de Nacre! Whilst the Côte de Nuits might end with a whimper, the Côte de Beaune may begin with a bang, for whilst the first village of Ladoix-Serrigny may not have built up a great reputation for wines under its own name, it plays host to vineyards producing a part of Corton-Charlemagne, one of the greatest white Burgundies, and also to some Corton blanc.

The relationship between the three appellations of Corton, Corton-Charlemagne and Charlemagne is confusing to even the most devoted student of Burgundy. The first thing that can be said is that no wine has been sold under the name of just plain Charlemagne for probably 30 years or more. That being so, would it not be an idea simply to suppress the appellation? It appears to have outlasted its usefulness. In any case all the vineyards which had the right to produce wine called Charlemagne can also make Corton-Charlemagne.

The confusion over the names of Charlemagne and Corton-Charlemagne is owed to a case of local Burgundian pride. It seems that when village boundaries were created in 1826, all the Charlemagne vineyard was given to the village of Aloxe, but that Pernand regained the major portion on appeal. In 1860, the then mayor of Aloxe, Louis Latour, proposed that the reputation of the vineyard would be increased by adding the name Corton to it, and this was accepted by decree two years later.

To increase the confusion the wine can be made not just from the vineyards called en Charlemagne in Pernand-Vergelesses and le Charlemagne in Aloxe-Corton, but also from le Corton, les Pougets and les Languettes in Aloxe-Corton. Thus, it is possible, quite legally, for a grower to make one wine which he could, at choice, call Corton-Charlemagne, Charlemagne or Corton blanc. In effect almost all the white wine from the three vineyard areas is called Corton-Charlemagne. These wines come from the vineyards at the top of the slope, circling the hillside just below the Bois de Corton. Where the vineyards lie parallel with the main road, the N 74, facing south-east, both red wines, under the name of Corton, and white, as Corton-Charlemagne, are produced, but when the vines curl round the slopes to face from south to north-west, then it is just white wines, the Corton-Charlemagne.

In an average year, about seventeen hogsheads of Corton blanc are also produced. For the most part this comes from parts of the Corton vineyard lower down the slope. Amongst these wines is the Corton-Vergennes Cuvée Paul Chanson of the Hospices de Beaune. This is a vineyard left to the Hospices in the early 1970s by Paul Chanson, one of Burgundy's great characters, who lived a bachelor life to the full and travelled around the world. Coincidentally, I have just received a brochure for country cottages in France to let. Amongst them is what was once his cottage at Bessey en Chaume, high up in the hills behind Savigny. It is described as being 'quite extraordinary, but has a charm of its own'. That, too, could have described Paul Chanson. Rather strangely he planted his white wine vineyards (he also had some Côte de Beaune) with Pinot Blanc grapes rather than the more usual Chardonnay. The Chandon de Briailles domain has also about a third of a hectare of Corton Bressandes producing white wine, with half planted in Chardonnay and half in Pinot Blanc.

Corton-Charlemagne takes its name from the Emperor, who used to have important vineyard holdings. There is an apocryphal tale that he planted the vineyards with white grapes at the request of his wife, because red wine stained his beard. It is unlikely however that she can have had too long to think about this problem, as he gave the vineyard to the abbey of Saulieu in 775 AD, when he was only 33 years old. Interestingly, the Charlemagne vineyard does not always appear to have made just white wine. There is a document dated 1674, which talks of a payment being made in Charlemagne both white and *clairet*, a kind of deep rosé wine.

For many lovers of white Burgundy the wines of Corton-Charlemagne come immediately after those of le Montrachet. Whilst it is perfectly dry, it has at the same time an appealing richness to its flavour. Because of the size of the vineyard and its variety of exposures to the sun and even soil styles, there can be a range of qualities, and it is useful to know the better growers. Henri Cannard, in his *Balades en Bourgogne*, says that the wine reaches its peak at about eight years old, but has a tendency to oxidise thereafter. Whilst there might be some truth in this, the implied criticism is part of what a Frenchman seeks from a white Burgundy. He seeks a wine that is totally crisp, whilst the English drinker often seeks a rounder, softer and, perhaps, slightly oxidised wine.

The most important owner in Corton-Charlemagne is the Bonneau de Martray domain, which is now managed commercially from Paris. In all they own almost an eighth of the total area, some 8.6 hectares. Their wines are invariably outstanding and they also have the reputation for making fine wines in what are generally considered to be 'off' years, though this is often a characteristic of the wines of the appellation. It is likely that the Bonneau de Martray holding is that which the Emperor Charlemagne himself owned more than twelve centuries ago.

The second holding in size is the seven hectares of Louis Latour. This the company purchased with the Château de Corton-Grancey and the magnificent press-house hewn into the hillside from the estate of the Comte de Grancey le

Château in 1891. The château had originally been built in 1749, by Charles Lébault, President of the Parliament of Burgundy. It is one of three châteaux in the village of Aloxe-Corton. The other two are the Château de Corton-André and the Château-Rolot, both built in the nineteenth century. Of all the wines that Louis Latour produce from their own vineyards, their Corton-Charlemagne is the one I prefer.

Two other Beaune merchant houses also have important pieces of Corton-Charlemagne. These are Bouchard Père et Fils with three hectares and Louis Jadot with 1½ hectares. Both are excellent wines.

Amongst the smaller growers who make excellent wine are Rapet Père et Fils (1.5 has) Dubreuil-Fontaine (1.33 has) and Hyppolite-Thevenot (0.5 has). The Hospices de Beaune, Cuvée Françoise de Salins, regularly one of the most expensive wines at the auction also comes from Corton-Charlemagne.

One of the other smaller owners in Corton-Charlemagne, though an important owner in Corton, is Louis Chapuis. In his book *Vigneron de Bourgogne*, he tells of the life of a grower in Aloxe-Corton over the years and recounts an amusing anecdote concerning one of his customers:

> How, for example could I be but touched by the fidelity of this octogenarian lady from Brittany, retired from a lifetime of teaching, who regularly ordered some Corton-Charlemagne to accompany her lobsters? Whenever she could, she came to Aloxe-Corton to enquire about the wine and to taste it from the cask. One evening, when the last bus had left, I could not take her to the station at Dijon. 'Stick convention,' she said, 'I'll hitchhike! I'm sure they'll stop more quickly when they see my white hair.'

Outside the *grand crus* of Corton-Charlemagne and Corton, there is little white wine produced in Aloxe-Corton. Following old traditions, three growers used to make a full-bodied supple wine from the Pinot Gris grape, but of these only the Daniel Sénard domain is apparently still producing a small amount from a plot of about 30 ares.

The village of Pernand-Vergelesses has a long tradition for its white wines outside those of Corton-Charlemagne. Especially well known were its Aligotés, and until as recently as 1948, a proportion of Aligoté could also be used in the making of Corton-Charlemagne. A number of the vineyards up behind the village have ideal soil for the production of white wine as does the *premier cru* les Caradeux, where Chanson Père et Fils make the only white wine of their domain. Another white Pernand, which won an informal competition as the best white Burgundy to match Colchester oysters, came from the vines of Jacques Germain based at Chorey les Beaune. The Laleure-Piot domain also makes excellent white wines from the village.

The villages of Savigny and Chorey are much better known for their red wines than for their whites, though about 400 hectolitres of white Savigny are made each year, much from the Pinot Blanc rather than the Chardonnay. Amongst the producers are Capron-Manieux and Jean Chénu. I have the feeling that a fair proportion of the total production is consumed at the local restaurant, l'Ouvrée.

An *ouvrée* is the local, traditional measurement of area which is still widely used by the growers. As Louis Chapuis says, 'The *vignerons* have always preferred human measurements to those imposed by the Republic.' It is based on the notional area that a man can work in a day and is just one of a series of Burgundian measurements. Eight *ouvrées* go to make a *journal* and this itself is made up of 860 *perches*. In modern day terms an *ouvrée* is 428 square metres. If you buy vineyard land in Burgundy, even today, there is little chance that it will be quoted in hectares or square metres; you will most probably be sold *ouvrées*.

Whilst the production of white wine in Beaune is less than that of Savigny, its reputation is much higher, mainly because of just one wine, the Clos des Mouches of Joseph Drouhin. In all, he owns about 13 hectares of this *premier cru*, which lies at the southern extremity of the vineyards of Beaune, adjoining those of Pommard, on the slopes of Mont Désiré. About half of the holding is planted in Chardonnay and it makes an outstanding wine with a flavour redolent of toasted hazelnuts. Fermentation takes place in oak hogsheads and ageing is mainly in new oak. Naturally such attention makes for an expensive wine, but it is one that merits the investment. It is arguable that it merits *grand cru* status, for it is consistently better than many wines that bear it. It shows the advantage of a monopoly situation, when there is a perfectionist in charge. This monopoly will not last long for Chanson Père et Fils have planted part of their holding in Clos des Mouches in Chardonnay. It will be sold as Clos des Mouches Mont Saint Désiré.

One other wine that one comes across regularly is the Beaune du Château blanc of Bouchard Père et Fils. This is made from their own holdings in the *premier cru* vineyards of Beaune and always appears without a vintage. I have also recently tasted from the same domain a Beaune Clos Saint Landry of the 1985 vintage, which had great depth of taste and was a most enjoyable discovery. The only other white Beaune that I have ever tasted is one made by the Hospices de Beaune. Apparently this is never offered at auction, due to the limited quantity made each year, but is kept back for official functions. The bottle I tasted had a most agreeable Chardonnay flavour and plenty of fruit.

Not to be confused with either Beaune or Côte de Beaune Villages, is the appellation Côte de Beaune. This can be used for any of the wines of Beaune itself, plus an additional 51 hectares on the hillside and in the valleys on the west of the town. Like Charlemagne, this is an appellation that has become largely redundant for despite the expected appeal of its name, comparatively little wine is produced. This includes about 40 casks a year of white wine. The one that I have tasted is the Clos des Pierres Blanches, made from Pinot Blanc, by Paul Chanson. Serena Sutcliffe also recommends that of the Lycée Agricole at Beaune, and I see that the Joliette domain sells a wine under the name of the Domaine des Pierres Blanches, which is presumably from the vineyard that previously belonged to Paul Chanson.

South of Beaune there comes a gap where nothing but red wine is produced. Both Pommard and Volnay now make no white wine, though in the eighteenth century up to one in eight vines in Volnay was Chardonnay. The grapes were also pressed through layers of straw to take away the colour and the Volnay of those days must have resembled today's blush wines from California.

Beyond Volnay comes the village of Monthélie, where the production of white wine is negligible and I must admit to never having seen a bottle. Beyond there begins the white wine country of the Côte d'Or, including the great village of Meursault, Puligny-Montrachet and Chassagne-Montrachet, which have already been dealt with in their own chapters. However there are many lesser villages producing white Burgundies which, whilst they might not enjoy the high reputations of their illustrious neighbours, often represent better value for money. The first of these is Auxey-Duresses. When Hubrecht Duijker first brought out *De Grote Wijnen van Bourgogne* in 1977 (in English, *The Great Wines of Burgundy*, 1983) he felt that the wines of Auxey-Duresses did not enjoy the reputation that they might. Too many growers were happy to make wines of mediocre quality; the reds for blending off as Côte de Beaune Villages and the whites as Bourgogne blanc. Since then much has changed. Every village with a right to sell under its own name has sought to build it up and thus receive higher prices. The white wines of Auxey are now in demand.

As far as reputation is concerned, the fact that the merchant Leroy, amongst the finest in Burgundy, is based in Auxey-Duresses, and owns 1½ hectares of vines in the village, is a big help. Another famous domain which makes and promotes the wine of Auxey-Duresses is that of the Duc de Magenta with 5 hectares. His whites are amongst the best that the village produces. Not far behind comes Robert Ampeau, who is better known for his wines from Meursault. The local list of growers include a number of members of the Prunier family, but the wines of Michel are probably the best ones to seek out. The Guillemard-Pothier domain from Meloisey also makes an Auxey-Duresses that I have regularly enjoyed.

The white wine vineyards of Auxey-Duresses are for the most part on the left-hand side of the road as it comes from

Meursault. They face in the strange direction, for Burgundy, of north-north-east. The wines lack the complexity and depth of flavour of the wines of Meursault, though in the best years they resemble them — and indeed were sold under that name for many centuries. They often have more acidity and can be rather two-dimensional.

Further up the same valley is the village of Saint Romain, which for a long time was considered to be part of the Hautes-Côtes. Historically, it is one of the most important villages of Burgundy, with remains going back to prehistoric times. The village is split into two parts; the older is clustered about the château, the origins of which are obscure. It existed at the beginning of the twelfth century and was bought by the Dukes of Burgundy in 1300 A.D. For more than a century they used it as their regional wine cellar, before selling it on to Philippe Pot, who already owned the Château de la Roche-pot. The château was destroyed during the French Revolution. In the meantime the village had spread into the valley bottom around the main road. Effectively, then, there are now two villages of Saint Romain. Apart from its vineyards, the village is also known for its cooperage, whose casks you are now as likely to see in California as Burgundy.

As has already been said, Saint-Romain for long produced Hautes-Côtes wines, and there is no doubt that there is where it belongs geographically. However, the ideal soil and the good positioning of many of its vineyards gave its wines a higher reputation, which was rewarded with its own *appellation contrôlée* in 1947. Originally nearly all the wine that was made was white, for the soil is chalky and the vineyards are rather higher up than is ideal for red wines, but in the early 1970s, the growers had difficulty in selling their wine so began planting Pinot Noir. However the full circle has turned and the white wines are now much more in demand, with companies such as Ropiteau Frères of Meursault helping with their promotion as a replacement for the more fashionable, and expensive, great white wine names of the Côte d'Or.

The village has been fortunate in having as its herald its long-time grower, poet and mayor Roland Thévenin. His verses, and the fact that he owned the Domaine des Moulin

107

aux Moines at Auxey-Duresses, the château at Puligny and a portion of le Montrachet, gave much reflected glory to the wines of Saint-Romain. One feels that it was not just in his role of mayor of the village, but also as a poet, that he wrote, 'As for the white wines of Saint Romain ... they are as delicate as a girl of sixteen years. They have that hearty freshness that can be seen on the face and in the eyes of all the young maidens of our Côte.' (It must be pointed out that Monsieur Thévenin has also had the reputation of being able to recognise a pretty girl when he saw one.)

Without reaching the fullness or the distinction of a Meursault or a Puligny-Montrachet, they are the ideal starting wine for any quality meal, knowing how to stimulate our taste-buds in preparation for the full attack of the great master wines.

They are always full of fruit and attraction, last well, and always ready to offer more than they have promised.

As well as the wines of Monsieur Thévenin, those of Fernand Bazenet and René Thévenin-Monthelie can be recommended. Whilst it is rare to see a vineyard name mentioned, the best for white wines are Sous Roches and Combe Bazin.

The next valley south from Saint-Romain has for centuries been one of the main routes of Burgundy. In Roman times the road led from the city of Augustodunum (Autun) to the valley of the Saône, and eventually the Rhine. More recently the main road from Paris to the Mediterranean, the N6, has swept down it and it was only by frantic lobbying that the motorway was diverted elsewhere to chew its way through the vineyards of Beaune and Savigny rather than through Montrachet. In this valley lies the village of Saint-Aubin, with its red and white wines. Incorporated within its limits is the hamlet of Gamay, which gave its name to a grape variety that over the centuries has done more to promote conversation and argument than anything else in Burgundy.

Whilst the village has about 170 hectares of vines, less than a fifth of them are used for the making of white Saint-Aubin, whilst almost as much again is planted in Aligoté. Peculiarly for the Côte d'Or, the vineyard names have been amalgamated from some 30 or so traditional ones, to some 16 that are used nowadays. Those producing the best white wines lie to the south-east of Gamay, up on the hillside, next to the vineyards of Puligny-Montrachet. The names to look out for are en Gamay, la Chatenière, les Murgers and les Dents de Chien. The chalky, stony nature of the soil is called up by the names les Dents de Chien, dog's teeth, and les Murgers, which is the Burgundian word for stones dug up in the vineyard and thrown to one side.

Some Burgundy lovers feel that the wines of Saint-Aubin are the most under-rated in the region, for the reason that the growers there take more pride in what they produce than in most other villages. It is also true that there seem to be a number of younger growers who have been prepared to adopt new techniques to improve the quality of their wines. It has been of help that there is a merchant in the village who has been happy to promote the wines not only of his own domain, but also the village wines in general. The company of Raoul Clerget makes some excellent wines at reasonable prices. Of the growers, there are a number of members of the Lamy family, with the Domaine Jean Lamy et ses Fils, now represented in Saint-Aubin by Hubert Lamy. Father Jean was, for years, the chairman of the association for the promotion of the wines of Saint-Aubin and the part that he played in the creation of their reputation has been important. A good Saint-Aubin is probably as closer in style to a wine from Chassagne-Montrachet than to one from Meursault or Puligny as it normally lacks the body of the former and the finesse of the latter.

After the two villages that share the name of Montrachet, Chassagne and Puligny, comes, in production terms, one of the most important villages of the Côte d'Or, Santenay. Only the villages of Gevrey-Chambertin, Beaune and Chassagne-Montrachet have a larger crop. It is true, however, that the soil is much better suited to the making of red wines than white for it is generally low in chalk and the local growers claim that the Chardonnay has difficulty in setting its fruit in the local vineyards. As a result, less than 5 per cent of the crop is white wine. Nevertheless an excellent white wine is made in the *premier cru* vineyard of les Gravières. The Clos des Gravières white is sold by the local *négociant* Prosper Maufoux, whose white wines generally are amongst the finest in Burgundy. It will match body with a most complicated palette of tastes.

For those who have experienced the stresses of tasting round the cellars and restaurants of Burgundy, Santenay offers an alternative attraction. It is a spa, whose waters, according to the local information bureau, are ideal for the treatment amongst other things, of all digestive problems, gout, obesity and stress as a result of living in the world of today. I am reliably informed that the taste of the waters is amongst the most unpleasant in France, but that is perhaps the price we must pay. A fringe benefit is that if you are a spa in France, you can have a casino — and Santenay boasts the forty-fourth largest, out of 150, in the country.

With Santenay, the white wine production of the Côte de Beaune effectively comes to an end. Whilst the three villages of Cheilly, Dezize and Sampigny-les-Maranges have the right to produce a white wine under the name of their respective village, during the past 15 years little has been sold as such. Their vocation would seem to have been largely to produce full-bodied red wines to beef up merchants' blends of Côte de Beaune Villages. Whatever white wine they might have produced will probably have been sold either as Bourgogne blanc, or to be sparkled.

Up in the hills lying behind, and running parallel to the vineyards of the Côte d'Or, is the Arrière-Côte. This is a hilly, beautiful countryside, named at one time by an unimaginative tourist promoter as the Burgundian Switzerland. For the visitor who has time to break away from the Route des Grands Crus, the scenery is often breathtaking and the restaurants are much cheaper! On a clear day, the view from the cliffs at Orches takes in Saint-Romain in the foreground, the valley leading down to Auxey-Duresses and Meursault, the valley of the Saône and occasionally the Alps.

In this region the vineyards are intermingled with pasture, woods, plantations of soft fruit and small villages. Because the climate is somewhat harsher, only certain slopes are planted with vines. Historically, this has been the region for the Aligoté as far as white wines are concerned, but during recent years there has been much planting of Chardonnay and, in one or two cases, of Pinot Gris, or Pinot Beurot, as it is known locally.

The most important expansion of the vineyards in the Hautes-Côtes has been carried out by the Nuits Saint Georges house of Geisweiler, at Bévy, some ten kilometres up in the hills to the west. There they bought almost 800 parcels of land to create a domain of 75 hectares of which slightly more than 20 are planted in Chardonnay, on soil which, according to official analysis, resembles that of Corton Charlemagne. The resultant wine is a typical, clean Chardonnay. As Philippe Léglise said in the local newspaper, a 'model of its type'.

As replanting for *appellation contrôlée* wines in Burgundy is only allowed where there have traditionally been vineyards, there are great possibilities for the Hautes-Côtes, for this is, once again, a region which had extensive plantings until the arrival of phylloxera. It is true to say that the Pinot Noir has been much more widely planted than white varieties, but a number of interesting wines, apart from the Cuvée Bévy, are being made.

Also in the Hautes Côtes de Nuits at Marey-les-Fussey is the Maison des Hautes-Côtes, a showpiece restaurant for the wines and other products of the region. It is an excellent place for a light meal at reasonable prices. The chairman of the committee responsible for it is Bernard Hudelot, who also makes an excellent Chardonnay at his domain at Villars Fontaine. More of a speciality is the Pinot Beurot wine made by, as far as I know, just two growers, Guillemard-Dupont at Meloisey (Hautes-Côtes de Beaune) and Thévenot Lebrun, from one of the few named vineyards, the eight hectare Clos du Vignon at Marey-les-Fussey.

About a quarter of the production of the wine from the Hautes-Côtes is carried out by the area's own co-operative cellar, which lies on the main road to the south of Beaune. Not only does it vinify the basic Hautes-Côtes wines, the Aligotés, the Passetousgrains, but also small quantities of a broad variety of other appellations, for many of the growers with vines in the Arrière-Côtes also own small plots in the more fashionable villages of the Côte itself. Founded in 1968, this cellar now has 115 members, and produces excellent wines which have won a number of awards. In 1970, the cellar signed an agreement giving exclusive distribution of its wines to the Savigny merchants Henri de Villamont, a part of the Swiss-owned Schenk wine-group, but somehow this seems to have fallen into abeyance, as the cellar now sells widely under its own label. Nevertheless, de Villamont played an important role in establishing the reputation of the wines of the Hautes-Côtes on both the French and export markets.

In one way, the wines of the Hautes-Côtes were trend-setters; when the legislation for the appellation was settled in 1961, it was decided that it would only be granted after tasting and analysis of the wine. Now, over 90 per cent of the samples submitted pass the test. It is also interesting to note that approximately half the production comes from vines planted in the Lenz Moser system, which originated in Austria, that is with the rows of vines further apart and trained much higher.

Increasing demand from around the world has meant that the consumer has had to pay more for the great wines of Burgundy. Whilst a bottle of Meursault in the past may not have been an everyday affair, it was affordable. Now many of us are having to look elsewhere for the taste of Chardonnay. It is not always necessary to look outside Burgundy. Whilst the novelty whites of the Côte de Nuits are expensive, there are still bargains to be had with such wines as Saint-Aubin and Auxey-Duresses, not to mention the wines of the Hautes-Côtes. Not only are the growers in these places becoming more commercially minded, but also the merchants are waking up to the fact that they must fill some of the holes in their offerings of white Burgundies. The increasing awareness of these 'lesser' white wines is one of the things for which we must all be grateful.

10
The Côte Chalonnaise

Traditions die hard in Burgundy and despite the efforts that have been made over many years to replace the name for the vineyards that lie at the northerly end of Saône et Loire *département*, the Côte Chalonnaise it remains. There are those who have flirted with the term the *Région de Mercurey*. I must admit to the fact that I have tried it myself, but somehow it seems unsatisfactory. The viticultural history of Chalon-sur-Saône may be in the past, and that of Mercurey very much in the present, but I feel much happier with the Côte Chalonnaise. Apart from its historical standing, the expression has a certain independence. It does not raise one village of the region on a pedestal above the others. It takes the historical capital of the area and recognises its majesty. The final decison has just been made in that Côte Chalonnaise has received the seal of approval with the new appellation for many of its wines Bourgogne Côte Chalonnaise.

Chalon's long vinous history is not in doubt. Long before the Romans came to Gaul, it was an important stage in the tin road from the mines of Cornwall to the eastern Mediterranean. Here boats were loaded with tin which had been shipped up the Seine and Yonne rivers and transported on land across the hills of the Morvan to the valley of the Saône and its onward journey. We know that wine was used to pay for both the transportation and the tin, so it is more than likely that much passed through the port of Chalon. In later days it was a centre of the Burgundy wine trade. Town records show that in 1479, the local wine sold for eight niquets a pint. (The niquet was a Burgundian coin made from copper. Due to speculative abuse it was withdrawn by François I in 1538.) In 1703 half a hogshead of white wine was sent by the local authorities in Paris to the Jesuits, as a thank-you for a thesis that had been dedicated to them. The trade must have been well developed for there are a series of local regulations controlling the sale. For example, in 1636, it was decreed that new wine could not be sold by the jug, and in 1765, that the white wine of the new vintage could not be sold before 12 November, Saint Martin's Day. Apart from its trading importance in wine, Chalon has been a centre of the fur trade since Roman times, and has had two fairs a year, nominally at least with this as the object, since the middle of the thirteenth century.

However important Mercurey might be in the world of wine, Chalon has always been a centre of international standing. The Emperor Constantine visited it frequently and considered it to be a town of good omen after he once had a miraculous vision there. With such imperial support I stick with the Côte Chalonnaise!

In many ways, the commercial history of the area in the wine trade shows similarities with that of Chablis. In both, river communications guaranteed distribution of the wine; in the case of Chablis, to Paris and the north, with the wines of the Côte Chalonnaise to Lyons and the Mediterranean. Both areas were more heavily planted with vines before the arrival of phylloxera than they are now. Both have, over the last 15 years, received much external investment and there has been much replanting. The wines of Mercurey, Rully, Givry and Montagny have never, however, managed to capture the imagination of the world to the extent that those of Chablis have, and there has never been the extra profit to reinvest that international prestige brings.

In historical terms, we are lucky that one of the great specialist books on Burgundy, *Les Vins du Beaujolais, du Mâconnais et Chalonnais*, by V. Vermorel and R. Danguy, was written just as the full effects of phylloxera were being seen. In Givry, for example, the disease destroyed more than 450 hectares of vines in the village, over 80 per cent of the total. Some 300 hectares were immediately replanted on to grafted rootstock. The proportion that was replanted was high, for the wines of Givry had enjoyed a good reputation for many centuries and sold easily. In less fashionable villages, much less replanting was carried out. In the village of Nanton, near to Sennecey-le-Grand, only a little more than a quarter was replanted and nearly all that in American hybrid vines.

The Great War, too, had a devastating effect on the villages of the region, with almost a total generation of winegrowers losing their lives — and their descendants their inclination. Much vineyard land was allowed to go fallow and some reverted to scrubland, only to be replanted in vines during the past few years.

Geographically, the Côte Chalonnaise is a continuation of the Côte d'Or, with the best vineyards facing east, south-east and occasionally south. The soil, too, is similar, with white wine vineyards, for the most part, being planted on chalky clay. There is not, however, a continuous strip of vineyards as there is on the Côte d'Or, but a constantly changing vista of vines, woods, meadows, quarries and scrubby hillsides. The vineyards are also set well back from the main road, so one has much less impression of being in a noted wine-producing region. In the area there are a number of merchants, with Antonin Rodet of Mercurey being one of the most important in Burgundy, one major co-operative cellar at Buxy, and a number of growers.

Whilst there are five village appellations, much of the area is given up to making generic wines like Bourgogne Grand Ordinaire and Bourgogne Aligoté. Indeed the village of Bouzeron, right at the north end of the Côte, has such a reputation for its Aligotés that since the spring of 1979, it has had its own appellation, Bourgogne Aligoté Bouzeron. This is an attempt to upgrade the image of the Aligoté, which is normally considered to be a Cinderella grape in Burgundy. Interestingly, the maximum production figure per hectare is generally the same as that for the white wines of villages like Puligny-Montrachet; 25 per cent less than that of the generic wine. The average production each year is just over 125,000 bottles.

Bouzeron has had a long reputation for its wines. In 872 AD, the village was given to a monastic order by Charles the Bald, which established a viticultural holding, which is still remembered by a local plot of land known as the Clos des Moines. At the beginning of the last century, Jullien describes its wines as having 'a distinguished taste which makes them approach the lesser wines of Meursault'. Later in the same century Danguy talks of their high reputation and their ability to last well.

One reason why the wines of the village enjoy such a high reputation is that there are some eminent owners in the village. These include the de Villaine family, who are co-proprietors of the Domaine de la Romanée-Conti and Bouchard Père et Fils, whose holding of five and a half hectares dates back to the last century. The one vineyard name that one comes across occasionally is the Clos de la Fortune of Chanzy Frères.

The village of Rully has had a strategic importance since the earliest of times, and the Barons de Rully were proud of the fact that they controlled three different castles in the one commune. However there was also one other local reputation, that of sickness, and as early as the twelfth century there was a medical asylum in the village. Many of the inhabitants died of the plague in 1347 and there were as few as twelve survivors. They abandoned their houses, dedicated the bodies and possessions to Saint Roch and Saint Sebastian and moved down the hillside to build a new village beside a clear-flowing spring.

Interestingly, St Roch himself died earlier in the same century and was renowned for healing those with the plague in northern Italy. Apparently, he is still invoked in France and Italy, where he is known as Rocco, in case of sickness.

Until the end of the last century, Rully was known for its red wines, but then the village became an important centre for the production of sparkling wines and it may be that the increase in production of white wines dates from then. Now there are rather more white wines made than red.

The village is the base of one of the most dynamic young men in Burgundy, its mayor, Jean-François Delorme. It seems that he has boundless energy and has rapidly built up an important business from the limited base of the vines of his father. He has the trading names of André Delorme and Meulien-Pigneret and the important holding of Côte Chalonnaise vines under the name of Domaine de la Renarde. In addition, for many years, he was chairman of the group of young Burgundy merchants, and is a tireless ambassador for the local wines, both still and sparkling.

His vineyard holdings now amount to over 60 hectares, most of them in Rully, but also to a much smaller extent in Mercurey and Givry. His pride is his monopoly vineyard Varot, 18 hectares reclaimed by him from scrubland. His success has caused some jealousy and his further expansion has been limited by the SAFER, a quasi-governmental body which supervises the distribution of vineyard holdings, theoretically to protect the interests of the smaller owners. Sadly this organisation has even prevented Jean-François from planting vines where nobody else was interested. (More amusingly its activities have also led to Robert Drouhin's daughter becoming a vineyard owner, with an independent mind!) His wines are classic Rullys with plenty of fruit and flavour, though perhaps lacking a little of the depth of the better wines of the Côte d'Or. In his imposing recently-contructed press-house and cellar there is a significant proportion of new wood used, which represents a major investment for a domain of this size. There is also the possibility of tasting perhaps the broadest range of single-vineyard wines from the Côte Chalonnaise under one roof.

Of the other growers in the village, the one whose wines I probably know best is Armand Monassier, who used to own the Paris restaurant, Chez les Anges, well known for its fine Burgundian cooking. I have recently learnt that he has now sold his vines. More frequently seen are the wines of the Domaine de la Folie. These vineyards overlook the local town of Chagny, perhaps best known for its outstanding restaurant Lameloise. There was much dispute as to whether the Domaine de la Folie lay within the boundaries of the Rully appellation, but Monsieur Nöel-Bouton, the owner, won the day and his white Clos Saint Jacques is certainly worthy of the appellation. The wines of the only remaining Château de Rully can be excellent and it is also worth looking out for wines from the Grésigny and Rabource vineyards of the Domaine Pierre Marie Ninot and the les Cloux and Rabource of the Santenay-based Domaine Saint-Michel, in which Pierre Maufoux has an interest.

To the south of Rully is the best-known appellation of the Côte Chalonnaise, Mercurey. Indeed its reputation is such that, for many years, it was a generic name for all the wines of the area and it was not until 1923, when an application by the growers of Givry and Rully to have the position legally formalised, was rejected by the courts that it was finally able to create its own reputation for its wines. The red wines of Mercurey have for many years been sold at prices that equal those of such Côte d'Or villages as Santenay and Pernand-Vergelesses. The fact that two of the major Côte d'Or merchants, Faiveley and Bouchard Aîné et Fils, have important vineyard holdings in the appellation also gives the wines a broader exposure than they might otherwise have. I have said in the appellation rather than in the village because the wine comes not only from Mercurey itself, but also from the two neighbouring villages of Bourgneuf Val d'Or and Saint-Martin-sous-Montaigu.

The Roman road that ran from Autun to Chalon runs through Bourgneuf and it is probable that there was in the locality a shrine to the god Mercury, and it is from this that the village takes its name.

The village is one of the first in Burgundy to have a book written about its wines. Surprisingly *Mercurey et ses Vins* was published in Bordeaux in 1883. The writer was a local grower Adalbert Mathey, who must have been widely read as there are numerous quotations from the local Biarritz paper! Also surprisingly, there is not a single mention of Mercurey producing white wines, though the production then, as now, represented about 5 per cent of the total.

The fact is that white wines in Mercurey are of secondary importance, though given the importance of the total production of the appellation, they still represent about 12,000 cases a year, which is about a third of the white wine production of Rully. An official publication of the Chevaliers du Tastevin describes the wines as being 'clean, warm and lively with a bouquet. The white wines of Mercurey deserve their great reputation and should be drunk young.' The same booklet says of the white Rullys, 'Full-bodied wines with finesse and a big bouquet, figuring among the very good growths of Burgundy.' Whilst the writer is scarcely permitted to be seen taking a position between the wines of rival villages, in my mind, at least, there is little doubt as to which of the two wines he prefers.

Notwithstanding what I have just written, Mercurey is capable of producing some most enjoyable white wines and I would particularly recommend that of the Château de Chamirey, the property of the Marquis de Jouennes d'Herville, who is also the owner of the wine company Antonin Rodet, which has a broad range of wines from all parts of Burgundy, not just the Côte Chalonnaise. (Perhaps this is the moment to mention the other local general Burgundy merchant, Emile Chandesais at Fontaines, near Rully, which is still run by the man who founded it over 50 years ago.) The Domaine Michel Juillot also regularly produces an excellent white Mercurey.

Pierre Andrieu tells of a tradition in Burgundy that the inhabitants of each village used to be known by a particular nickname; that for the people of Mercurey was *les Glorieux*. Apparently this had rather more the meaning of 'proud' than 'glorious'. This pride in their wines is continued by their own selection of the best wines of the village, which now bear the label of the 'Disciples of the Chante Flute'. I must admit that I do not know quite who or what they follow, but their wines have a steady, if largely local, following.

The local tourist office has a special leaflet about the road from Chagny to Cluny. Both Rully and Mercurey lie to the west of this road, but the next village giving its name to an *appellation contrôlée* lies firmly on that route. To reach Givry from Mercurey one can take the main road towards Chalon sur Saône and then turn south on the tourist route, or a more pretty way is by the valley of the Orbise and the village of Barizey, which has a small co-operative cellar with regularly open tasting facilities. During the last century, this village was thought to lie above rich seams of both coal and gypsum and, at the time of phylloxera, there must have been a strong temptation to abandon the vineyards totally.

Givry is yet another village whose reputation is firmly based on its red wines, which were reputedly appreciated by Henri IV, who may have valued Paris at a Mass, but is not recorded as having put a price on the wines of Givry. It is fair to say that he did have certain intra-mural interests in the neighbourhood, as he had a more than passing interest in the local beauty, Gabrielle d'Estrées. On the strength of this attraction the wines of Givry often bear the slogan, 'le vin préferé de Henri IV'. One of the shippers to use such a label is the Beaune house of Remoissenet Père et Fils, who have always featured the wines of Givry. One of their reasons for doing this is their close connection with the village's most famous grower, Baron Thénard, a real press-baron, if only on a regional scale. As he is also one of the most important owners of le Montrachet, his name commands respect wherever he goes in the wine world.

The total production of white Givry in an average year is approximately 500 hectolitres, just over 5,000 cases. The number of producers of white Givry is therefore very limited. Apart from Baron Thénard's wine, I can only remember having tasted a Clos du Cellier aux Moines of André Delorme, but Serena Sutcliffe also recommends the white wines of the Maurice Derain and Ragot domains.

The village of Givry has a long viticultural history. A decree of Philippe de Valois in 1349 fixed the entry duties of a cask of its wine into Paris at six sous, three times as much as the then fashionable wines of the Loire. Also in the fourteenth century, the town was permitted to encircle itself with fortifications, but these seem to have proved to be an attraction to an assortment of private armies and within the next two and a half centuries, it was sacked on at least three occasions, most seriously in 1576, when most of it was destroyed by fire.

The final appellation of the Côte Chalonnaise is that of Montagny, which comes not just from the village of that name but also from the small town of Buxy and the neighbouring villages of Saint-Vallerin and Jully-les-Buxy. The appellation is applied only to white wines, but there is one distinction that applies to no other *appellation contrôlée* in Burgundy. Every single vineyard has *premier cru* status, if the wine has the necessary extra half degree of alcohol to bring it up to 11.5°.

There must have been some interesting discussions around the time that the appellation was created in 1936, for until then most of the local wine was red and sold under the name of Côte de Buxy. That there should be this dramatic change from red to white wines and that the name which meant something to the consumers, Buxy, should be sacrificed, suggests a great deal of lobbying by the growers of Montagny. It is fair to say that the village of Montagny is surrounded by vines, whilst Buxy stands slightly apart, but nevertheless I feel certain that at some meeting 50 years ago, there must have been a well-planned coup.

Like most of those of the Côte Chalonnaise, the Montagny vineyards are not in one block. They are spread out in small parcels amongst the villages. The area is one of small hills and the vines planted on these are less likely to suffer from spring frosts and fogs which can lead to the grapes failing to develop. Whilst there is a list of some 64 vineyard names authorised, these are not often seen, as the wine is generally sold as Montagny or Montagny *premier cru*. Two properties that are seen however are the Château de la Saule and the Château de Davenay. The former, belonging to the Roy-Thévenin family, makes a typical quality Montagny, full-bodied and with a hint of richness that one does not find normally in a Rully. The Château de Davenay on the hillside above Buxy has belonged for some years to the Gilardoni family and has been falling slowly into disrepair. Recently, it has been leased by Picard Père et Fils, a fast expanding company based in Chagny. They are committed to improving the quality of the wine and to bottling at the Château, which has also in the past produced Bourgogne rouge, Bourgogne Passetousgrains and Bourgogne Aligoté, as well as Montagny. It is very probable that little of these last two wines

121

will be made in the future. In the past the Nuits Saint Georges house of Moillard has bought much of the Château de Davenay Montagny and sold it under its own label. This arrangement has now come to an end.

Picard Père et Fils have also shown their commitment to the Côte Chalonnaise by buying a local wholesaler at Buxy, G. Romann, who bottle and sell a broad range of wines. They consider as their rivals La Cave des Vignerons de Buxy, by far the most important co-operative cellar of the Côte Chalonnaise, which has built up a big reputation for its wines, both on the domestic market and abroad. In a recent tasting of economically priced Burgundies their Montagny *premier cru* 1985 showed particularly well. However, much of their success has been as a source for the lesser wines of Burgundy, such as Bourgogne Aligoté, Passetousgrains and Grain Ordinaire. This has meant that many of the 'house Burgundies' one meets come from this cellar. They are also producers of sparkling wines. This is one of the co-operative cellars to show that rigorous selection of raw material, and encouragement of local growers, can lead to excellent wines at reasonable prices.

Whilst the co-operative cellar at Buxy has done much to enhance the reputation of the wines of Montagny, much has also been done by the prestigious Beaune company Louis Latour. For many years now, they have entered the market shortly after the vintage and bought up the best Montagnys they can find for eventual sale under their own label. Whilst they have been criticised by some of their competitors for inflating the wines of the Côte Chalonnaise by being prepared to pay a high price for the best wines, it is interesting to see that more and more of the traditional shippers from Beaune and Nuits Saint Georges are now showing interest in the wines from the Côte Chalonnaise. Whilst ten years ago they might for the most part have offered a Mercurey, now most of them list wines from the other villages. The fact is that the Côte Chalonnaise wines have remained reasonably priced when compared with the white wines of the Côte d'Or. No one would claim that an average Rully is as good as an average Puligny-Montrachet, but there is little doubt that it is as good as, for instance, an average Saint-Romain. There is room for increased production, but many of the growers are happy to grow Aligoté grapes. They can always find a ready outlet in the production of sparkling wine if the demand for Bourgogne Aligoté is not buoyant — though, as I write this, it is. The Chardonnay will be more widely planted when its wines can command an adequate premium. That moment is coming.

Sparkling wine is a major speciality of the Côte Chalonnaise with the village of Rully having a particular reputation for their production. There is no doubt that this industry has encouraged many of the local growers to leave their vineyards planted in Aligoté.

For the tourist, the Côte Chalonnaise is vastly different from the Côte d'Or. There is not the pressure that one has when one visits places with the best known tourist names. Eating is half the price and the growers seem to have a little more time to talk about their wines. There are a number of tasting cellars, of which perhaps the best are in Chagny and Buxy, if you cannot find your way in that of a grower.

For the consumer, frightened by current high prices, the wines of the Côte Chalonnaise are worth seeking out, be they under the name of a local producer or of a Côte d'Or merchant. It is in the areas like this that Burgundy must seek to expand its reputation, if it is to be appreciated by any but the wealthiest connoisseurs. For most wine drinkers the white wines of the Côte d'Or are luxury items to be appreciated rarely. Burgundy has however, in the Côte Chalonnaise good, and sometimes fine, wines at more affordable prices.

11
The Mâconnais and Beaujolais

The vineyards of the Mâconnais provide an important proportion of the bulk of the production of the white wines of Burgundy. In many ways, they are the white equivalent of the Beaujolais. It is almost certain that nine bottles out of ten of Bourgogne blanc will come from here, in addition to the large quantities of Mâcon and Mâcon-Villages.

Once again, the region takes its name from a peripheral town, for Mâcon lies to the south and east of the vineyards. The other limiting towns could be considered to be Tournus in the north and Cluny in the west, though there are vineyards outside this area further to the west, producing sound wines at the lower levels.

As a town, Mâcon has pleasurable memories for me, for it was here that I first met Burgundy, when I visited the National Wine Fair almost 30 years ago. Though I was a naive beginner in the trade, I was looked after by Jean Mommessin for three days in a manner that is hard to forget. There has been an annual wine fair in the town since at least 1340 and the extent to which tasting must have gone on is illustrated by the fact that it became known as the Foire Chaude or Hot Fair. The modern fair dates from 1933, when a group of growers came together in a bid to relaunch it. Now it is the *National* wine fair, where wines not just from France, but from around the world are judged. In status, a medal from the Mâcon fair probably comes second only to one from the Concours Agricole, though with something like

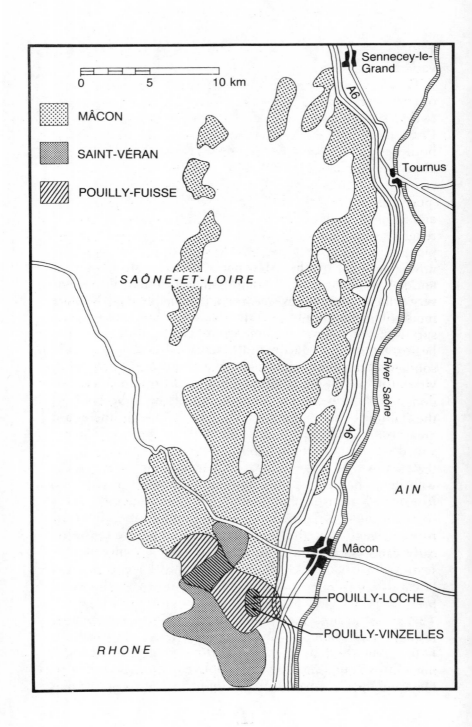

1,300 tasters on the judging panels there must be some variations in the quality of the decisions reached.

The main beauty of the town of Mâcon is its position, lying on the west bank of the river Saône, with an attractive twelve-arched bridge carrying the traffic across the river. Until the coming of the motorway, it was one of the worst bottlenecks on the road to the south. It is not a town that has always been admired. An English guidebook of just over a century ago dismissed the railway-station buffet as being 'poor' and the town 'a dull place'. It went on, 'Religious wars and revolutions have nearly denuded Mâcon of all its ancient religious structures, and within the last few years, even the picturesque old wooden houses have disappeared, and it is now a modern French town, with scarcely any vestige of antiquity visible.' It is true that its historical past is still not very evident, and even as a centre of the wine trade, it has lost much of its importance, with Mommessin the last major survivor of the 20 or so merchants based in the town at the beginning of the century. As a gastronomic capital for southern Burgundy, however, it is well placed, with the vineyards of the Beaujolais and the Mâconnais on the doorstep, the Bresse, with its chickens, across the river, and the Charollais, with its cattle, lying just beyond the vineyard area.

In an earlier book, I mentioned that Saint Valérian, one of the two patron saints of Tournus, picked up his head and walked away with it after he had been beheaded by the Romans for his beliefs. Rather simply, I imagined this to be something special, but subsequent reading has shown this not to be the case, though it did generally qualify the victim for early canonisation. Another son of Tournus is the painter Jean-Baptiste Greuze. According to Larousse his pictures had 'a clear moral intent — although they also had a tinge of preciosity, that gradually turned into more overt sensuality'. This artist is remembered in the name of an excellent local restaurant as well as in a museum. This was set up by a fervent admirer, himself an artist. Unfortunately finance did not run to exhibiting any original works of art by Greuze. However, more than 500 reproductions were on show.

Fortunately, thanks to the generosity of some benefactors, this situation has now been remedied and a number of his paintings are now on show. The pride of Tournus is undoubtedly the church of Saint Philibert, which was built at the beginning of the eleventh century, on the site of two earlier churches built by monks who had come from the island of Noirmoutier at the end of the ninth century.

Cluny was for many years the most important centre of Western Christianity after Rome. It was the headquarters of the Benedictine order, whose Abbot was answerable, in this world at least, to nobody but the Pope. Not only was Cluny a missionary centre (at the peak of its power it was reputed to control 2,000 monasteries) but it was also an important focal point of the architectural world, with accompanying schools of stonemasons, sculptors and iron-workers. The overheads must have been enormous, but there is an old rhyme which goes,

> En tous Pay ou le vent vente
> L'Abbé de Cluny a des rentes

Loosely translated, this might mean,

> In every country where the wind blows,
> The Abbot of Cluny's rent-collector goes.

Life cannot have been too hard, for it was as a protest against the lack of application of monastic principles that three monks, Robert, Albéric and the Englishman, Stephen Harding, left Cluny in 1098 to found the Cistercian order and to give the same impetus to wine production on the Côte d'Or that the monks of Cluny had given in the Mâconnais and the Beaujolais.

The abbey at Cluny, with its windows 100 feet tall, was a major victim of the French Revolution. It was sold off in bits and pieces and much of it was dismantled for use as building materials. Now part of it has found a new lease of life as a government school for Arts and Crafts.

Near to Cluny is Taizé, the centre of the international Christian ecumenical movement. The area between Cluny and Tournus is known not only for its wines, but also for a number of unspoilt Romanesque churches, mainly dating from the twelfth century.

Whilst we have seen already that there has been a general movement of production in Burgundy towards white wines, it is in the Mâconnais that this has been particularly noteworthy. At the end of the last century Danguy could write of the Mâconnais, 'Producing good *vins ordinaires* and excellent *vins fins*, this region has acquired a truly European reputation, and there is no part of the world where you cannot find Mâcons.' Yet the wines of which he was talking were almost totally red. The only villages whose names he mentions in connection with a reputation for white wines are Fuissé, Pouilly, Vergisson and Solutré. That white wine was made in some of the other villages is clear, but the quantity was only minimal. For example in the 1892 vintage the village of Chardonnay produced not a drop of white wine. In Igé, in 1889, there were 915 hectolitres of red wine made and only 10 of white. The one exception seems to be the village of Viré, where white wine accounted for 60 per cent of the production — and was able to sell for as much as a third more per hectolitre than the red. Perhaps a sign of things to come was the replanting the same year of the local 18-hectare property au Chapitre, which had once belonged to the Abbey of Cluny. The Ducloud family purchased it in 1888 and immediately replanted it, four-fifths in Chardonnay or Pinot Blanc on Riparia rootstocks, and the balance in Gamay.

Interestingly, the red wines of the Mâconnais had been made from the Pinot Noir, and these were the wines that became popular at the court of Louis XIV, as the result of some shrewd marketing by Claude Brosse, a local vineyard owner, whose size, and the quality of his wine, caught the attention of the king in 1660. Later the Pinot was replaced, as in so many places, by the Gamay, for the growers found that they could produce considerably more wine, with little extra effort.

As the Pinot Noir changed to the Gamay, so has the Gamay changed to the Chardonnay. Comparative statistics can be gained from two different editions of the classic reference book on Burgundy by Pierre Poupon and Pierre Forgeot. In 1952, the average annual production for red wines in the Mâconnais was put at 60,000 hectolitres, in 1985 at 45,600. The equivalent figures for all the white wines of the Mâconnais, including Pouilly-Fuissé and its satellites, have risen from 69,600 hectolitres to 159,400 hectolitres.

Within the region, the hierarchy of white wines is somewhat complicated. At the top of the tree comes the appellation Pouilly-Fuissé, followed by its lesser neighbours Pouilly-Vinzelles, Pouilly-Loché and Saint-Véran. Next come Mâcon-Villages and Mâcon-Supérieur and at the bottom plain Mâcon blanc or Pinot-Chardonnay-Mâcon. All these wines are made from the Chardonnay; for those wines with Mâcon in the title, the Pinot Blanc is permitted.

Much of the wine sold as plain Mâcon, or Pinot-Chardonnay-Mâcon, is produced by the co-operative cellars, of which there are a number in the region. Most of what they produce is then sold to the major merchants for bottling under their own label, though a greater proportion now seems to be sold under the label of the co-operative cellar itself. It is interesting that the local growers have taken vigorous steps to protect their appellation Pinot-Chardonnay-Mâcon. Although the decree authorising this term dates back to 1937, it is only in the past few years, with the increasing use, especially in the United States, of varietal names to label a wine, that its full worth has been appreciated. Attempts have even been made to forbid the appearance of either Pinot Chardonnay or Chardonnay on the labels of wines from elsewhere as the term was the exclusive right of the Mâconnais growers, written on the immutable stone tablets of the *appellation contrôlée* laws. Fortunately for the rest of the world, this claim has not proved successful.

A plain Mâcon blanc should be a simple, crisp wine with plenty of fruit and a pronounced varietal characteristic. Recently it has been selling at a lower price than Bourgogne Aligoté, which only goes to show how confused prices can become when production loses touch with demand.

More commonly seen on world markets nowadays is the appellation Mâcon-Villages. This can come from one or more of some 36 villages which produce the finest white wine in the Mâconnais. Frequently, when the wine comes from just one of those villages it will appear with the name of the village tacked on after Mâcon. Thus Louis Latour have built up a fine reputation for a wine sold as Mâcon-Lugny and Piat for a Mâcon-Viré. Often these wines come from the co-operative cellar of the village named and amongst those with good reputations are the cellars of Chaintré, Prissé, Clessé, Viré, Lugny and Chardonnay. This last village is not the only local one to give its name to a grape, for within the Mâcon-Villages region is the village of Chasselas. I imagine therefore that it would be quite legal, though rather confusing, to label a wine as Mâcon-Chasselas. One of the other villages is Milly, which has now added to its name not the name of its most famous vineyard, as it would have done if it had been on the Côte d'Or, but of its most famous inhabitant, the poet Lamartine.

The role of the co-operative cellars is one of the utmost importance in the production of the wines of the Mâconnais, as four-fifths of the wine made in the region passes through their hands. Comparatively little, though, is actually bottled by them, as three-quarters of the production is ultimately sold under the label of Burgundian merchants. On the spot sales, too, can be of importance. The co-operative cellar at Igé, for example, disposed of a quarter of its turnover at the 'farm-gate' though it is helped by having set up its stall in what used to be a chapel, built in the eleventh century by the monks of Cluny, in the village of Domange.

Whilst many of us recognise the merits of Lamartine as a poet, he wished to be considered as a *vigneron* and wine-merchant. Indeed, he liked to be known as the 'first winegrower in France' and the Burgundians have tried to profit to the maximum from his connection with the soil. His works have been pillaged unmercifully for quotations to describe wines on the one hand, and, on the other hand a certain Father Claudius Grillet, a professor at Dijon university, went so far as to produce a work entitled, *A Great*

Winemaker, Lamartine. History does not tell us too much of the quality of his wines, but it does give us a clear idea of his business sense. It was disastrous.

As I have already said, much of the wine from the Mâcon-Villages comes from the co-operative cellars. However, there is an ever increasing number of vineyard and growers names that are attracting the attention of the consumer. The Thévenet domain at Clessé is one outstanding example, with wines appearing under a variety of names, including Mâcon-Clessé, Mâcon-Villages Clessé, Thévenet-Wicart and Domaine de la Bon Gran. Other wines that I have enjoyed recently include the Mâcon-Viré, Domaine de Roally, Mâcon-Lugny, Domaine du Prieuré and the Mâcon-Uchizy of the Domaine Talmard. The village of Lugny has two vineyard names of note. Les Charmes, of over 80 hectares, lies on a plateau behind the village and is marketed by the local co-operative cellar, under a variety of qualities including a Vieilles Vignes. Close to it, but much smaller, is Les Genièvres, sold exclusively by Louis Latour. Another single vineyard with a high reputation is the two hectare Clos du Chapitre at Viré, belonging to the merchants Jacques Dépagneux. Also a very useful standby on a wine list is the Mâcon-Villages Laforêt of Joseph Drouhin.

Whilst one expects a Mâcon-Villages to be fuller in flavour and fruit than a normal Mâcon, one would scarcely expect one to be sweet. Indeed, this is not something that one would expect from any white Burgundy. Nevertheless the exceptional summer of 1983 enabled the Thévenet domain at Clessé to produce a botrytis wine in the Californian late-harvest style. I have no idea as to whether this was made deliberately by the grower or whether it came about by accident, but the result was a silver medal in the Sweet White class at the International Challenge of *Wine Magazine*, where the judges compared it to an old sweet wine from the Loire. Whilst, in the annals of Burgundy, it can be considered little more than a curiosity, it does show what can be done in exceptional circumstances, with good vinification.

It is perhaps at this level that one can find the best value for money in the white wines of Burgundy. A good Mâcon-

Villages will have a distinctive Chardonnay flavour, will be clean and refreshing and, in the best years, is capable of having some of the opulence and complexity that one would expect from the more noble wines of the Côte d'Or. As the production is high, qualities can and do vary, so it is, as elsewhere in Burgundy, often wise to rely on a good name, and pay more for it.

Saint-Véran is an appellation about which I have misgivings, for I feel that it was created for the wrong reasons. In the late 1960s, when the sales of Pouilly-Fuissé, particularly on the American market, began to take off, certain growers from neighbouring villages felt that they would like to increase the value of their wines by creating a new appellation. This came into effect in 1971 and applies to the following villages: Chânes, Chasselas, Davayé, Leynes, Prissé, Saint-Amour, Saint-Vérand and those parts of the vineyards of Solutré which do not have the right to produce Pouilly-Fuissé.

The reason why the name of the village of Saint-Vérand has a 'd' and the wine does not, is also something of a mystery. Hubrecht Duijker in his *The Great Wines of Burgundy* says that the village originally did not have a 'd' but that it was confused with a village of the same name in the south of the Beaujolais, next to le Bois de Oingt. As my map of the area also gives this village a final 'd', my confusion becomes even more intense. I can only imagine that the white wine has had the final 'd' *removed* to avoid confusion.

The situation is made no easier by the fact that the vineyards of Chânes, Chasselas, Leynes, Saint-Amour and Saint-Vérand also lie within the limits of the Beaujolais-Villages and the Mâcon-Villages. This means that there is a bewildering choice of names under which the growers can sell their wines. Thus an owner in Leynes, for example, could sell his white wine as Saint-Véran, Mâcon-Leynes, Mâcon-Villages, Beaujolais-Leynes, Beaujolais-Villages, Beaujolais Blanc, Mâcon Supérieur, Mâcon, Bourgogne or Bourgogne Grand Ordinaire and his red wines as Beaujolais-Villages, Beaujolais-Leynes, Beaujolais Supérieur, Beaujolais, Bourgogne Grand Ordinaire, and possibly Mâcon-Leynes, Mâcon

Supérieur and Mâcon. With just two wines of the right quality, one can establish a wine list of some importance.

As the growers previously sold much of their white wine as Beaujolais blanc, an important proportion of the total production of this has now disappeared, with the result that it has become rarer — and more expensive. Indeed, on many occasions since the introduction of the appellation, Saint-Véran has sold for a lower price than Beaujolais blanc, the appellation that previously did not sell dearly enough. It is a classic example of how fragmentation can increase prices. I suppose that this is good news for the growers, but not for us, the consumers.

In no way do I want to denigrate the quality of the wines of Saint-Véran. They form a bridge between the better Mâcon-Villages and the wines of Pouilly-Fuissé. They tend to have more body and depth than the former, but rather less than the latter. The production is quite substantial, almost twice as much as the total production of white wine of the four appellations of the Côte Chalonnaise.

One of the more prestigious of the producers in Saint-Véran is Marcel Vincent, who is rather better known as the owner of the Château de Fuissé. Of other growers whose wines I have tasted, I can recommend the 'les Cras' of Henri-Lucius Grégoire and those of the Duperron domain. The co-operative cellar at Prissé can always be relied on, as can the local school of viticulture, the Lycée Agricole at Davayé. As is so often the case in the region, much of the best wine appears under the label of Georges Duboeuf, whilst Mommessin market the Domaine de L'Evêque and Chanut Frères, the Domaine des Dîmes.

I must admit to a feeling of frustration as to how the *appellation contrôlée* system has developed in Burgundy. If I have expressed reservations about the independence of Saint-Véran, I have similar doubts about Pouilly-Loché and Pouilly-Vinzelles. It is not that they do not make good, and even, on occasion, great wine. It is more their size. Between them, their production is a fifth of that of Saint-Véran and because the local growers in Pouilly-Loché have the option of calling their wines Pouilly-Vinzelles, there have been a number of years when no Pouilly-Loché has been produced. Indeed, whenever I was lecturing, I always used to say that this was the invisible wine, for, during many years in Burgundy, I never came across it. Now my story is spoilt, for I tasted a wine that was labelled Pouilly-Loché for the first time a year ago, just 28 years since I first visited Burgundy. Since then, however, I have come across it on a number of occasions.

Whilst most of the wines of Loché and Vinzelles lack the fullness of a Pouilly-Fuissé, they are on the level of most of the wines of Saint-Véran. Whilst the vineyards are not contiguous with those of Saint-Véran (which fall into two separate and distinct parts), they would form a logical extension to them, almost completing the circle around the vineyards of Pouilly-Fuissé. Like the wines of Saint-Véran, the only grape variety allowed is the Chardonnay, but the yields are slightly smaller for Loché and Vinzelles than for Saint-Véran. (When this last appellation was created, all wines had to be submitted for tasting, but this is theoretically now the rule for all *appellation contrôlée* wines.)

The real reason why these minute appellations jealously maintain their privileged and separate status is that they have in their title the magical name Pouilly. This, they think, with some justification, is their passport to comparative riches. This gives them a standing on a wine list that they might not have if they joined their larger but much younger brother. Even Monsieur Bourdon, of the local co-operative cellar, admits that there is little justification for the continuance of the appellation Pouilly-Loché. Nevertheless the cellar is continuing to offer both Pouilly-Vinzelles and Pouilly-Loché. It is fair to say that the wines of the 1985 vintage were totally distinctive when tasted side by side recently, with the Loché having a pronounced nose of *herbes de Provence*. The committee of the cellar have taken the decision to concentrate on quality in the future and make efforts to have the appellation Pouilly-Vinzelles more appreciated in its own right, rather than as a Cinderella sister to Pouilly-Fuissé.

Vinzelles has an important place in history, as it was the senior barony under the Counts of Mâcon. In the reign of

Louis VII, one of these barons based himself at the castle of Vinzelles and made a good living by plundering the assets of the local church dignitaries. In less than 20 years, the Bishop of Mâcon, the Abbots of both Cluny and Tournus, and the Lord of Beauge all had to run to the king to seek redress. In 1172, he came in person to Vinzelles to sort out the matter. At the beginning of the fifteenth century, the castle was captured by the Duke of Suffolk after spirited resistance by 40 Lombard and Spanish mercenaries, who were garrisoning it.

The vineyards of Loché and Vinzelles are on a chalky hillside, facing east and thus ideal for the making of good wine. Despite their close relation to Pouilly, however, their wines have never managed to approach their more illustrious neighbour in price. At the end of the nineteenth century, the best white wine of Loché sold for 80 francs the hectolitre, whilst the lesser wines of Pouilly sold for 120 francs and the finest for 150 francs the hectolitre.

It is interesting that the villages of Loché and Vinzelles, in order to increase their reputation, have added neither the name of their most famous vineyard, nor that of their most famous inhabitant. Rather they have chosen that of a hamlet, which is on the land of neither of them, nor even on that of the next-door parish. The cynic might suggest that they are trying to profit from a reputation that is by no means theirs.

With vigorous fluctuations in the price of Pouilly-Fuissé, many of the merchants of Burgundy have sought to use Pouilly-Vinzelles as a replacement, with once again Georges Duboeuf often to the fore in buying the best *cuvées*. I have also recently enjoyed a wine from the Château de Vinzelles, sold by Loron, and Jean Mathias, a grower at Chaintré, makes a consistently good Pouilly-Vinzelles.

If it is possible to design the perfect setting for vineyards, then the architect would come up with something approaching those of Pouilly-Fuissé. They consist of a series of horseshoes facing in a south-westerly direction. Each of the horseshoes has steeply sloping sides, thus creating individual microclimates, purpose-made to catch and take full advantage of the sun.

The vineyards are spread between four different villages, Vergisson, Solutré, Fuissé and Chaintré. Pouilly itself is not more than a hamlet on the boundary between Solutré and Fuissé. The neighbourhood is dominated by two crags each approaching 500 metres high. These are the rocks of Vergisson and Solutré. For some strange reason the rock of Vergisson seems to have had little history attached to it, whilst that of Solutré goes back to prehistoric times, when some thousands of horses were driven over the edge to their death. There is a small museum in the village of Solutré dedicated to these and other prehistoric remains. In more recent times, the summit of the hill has been occupied by the sacrificial grove of druids, a Roman camp and a castle built by Raoul, Duke of Burgundy, who became king of France in 923 AD. Amongst the defending forces when the castle was besieged by Philippe le Bon in 1424 were 400 English soldiers. Apparently the fact that the castle was in the neighbourhood caused a considerable amount of local hardship and there was general rejoicing when it was razed to the ground in 1435.

Whilst one likes to think of the demand for Pouilly-Fuissé as being a recent phenomenon, the quality of the wines has been recognised for many years. Indeed during the last century, in general appreciations of the white wines of Burgundy, they were often considered after le Montrachet and the wines of Meursault. There is no shortage of praise. Jullien says of the wines of Pouilly, 'They are rich, with finesse, full-bodied agreeable and with plenty of nose, but overall they are alcoholic. With reason they are reproached for being too heady; one is wise to drink them only in moderation.' Some 40 years later, Dr Jules Guyot, in his report to the French Minister of Agriculture, writes, 'I have tasted white wines from Pouilly, Fuissé and Vinzelles, which yield little to the wines of Meursault and Puligny; they have body, perfume and delicacy.' Earlier in the same book, he says, 'Take as witness Pouilly, Fuissé, Vinzelles etc. with their essentially chalky soil, where the white wines from the Chardenay offer really remarkable qualities.' For an English appreciation, one can turn to Charles Tovey, who almost claims to have discovered the wines for the British market.

Pouilly, to which I made special reference in my first edition of 1862 is a wine of great merit. At Juliennes I have found Pouilly Fuissé, which turned out remarkably well. The white wines continue to improve by age whilst the red after twelve or fourteen years deteriorate . . . The inexperienced frequently get sold to them as Chablis the wines of Pouilly. I do not remember to have seen any quotation of Pouilly in circulars until my introduction to the wine in 1858, and I found in Burgundy that Pouilly was sent to England as Chablis. It is seldom found at the present time in quotations of Burgundy wines. A French dinner is usually preceded by oysters, which delicacies are saluted with a treble volley of Chablis, or, for greater solemnity, libations of Pouilly or Mont Rachet.

There is still much truth in what these Victorian writers had to say. Because of the richness of the micro-climates, the wines of Pouilly-Fuissé are regularly the strongest wines in Burgundy, a region noted, and often feared, for the strength of its wines. The wines have a soft exterior and rather less apparent acidity than their cousins from the Côte d'Or. This makes them easy to drink and a pitfall for the unwary. Nowadays their reputation does not put them on the same level as the wines of Montrachet, although their prices have often been amongst the highest of any white wine in Burgundy. During the summer of 1985, the price of a bottle of simple Pouilly-Fuissé rose to over 100 francs at the grower's cellar. For this the strong dollar and a weak franc were to blame. Within nine months the same bottle could be bought for approximately 35 francs. By this time the dollar had fallen sharply and the franc had strengthened. In the wines of Pouilly-Fuissé, which for some bizarre reason seem to have a hypnotic fascination for the American consumer, there has been more speculation, and more fingers burnt over the years than any other wine of Burgundy, with the possible exception of Chablis.

I would not like to decry the merits of the wines of Pouilly-Fuissé, but nowadays they are not worth twice as much as a good village wine from Meursault. That was the situation in which the trade found itself.

For the vines of Pouilly-Fuissé (and Loché and Vinzelles), only a local traditional form of pruning is permitted. This is the *taille a queue du Mâconnais*, with one to three shoots curved over and attached to the lower wire for training.

Each of the villages that go to make up the appellation has its own style of wine. Those of Fuissé are reputed to be the best, Solutré to be slightly coarser in style and those of Vergisson, to have rather more delicacy. As with many of the white wines of Burgundy, those of Pouilly-Fuissé are too often drunk young, before their full charm can be appreciated. As Jean Mommessin has written, 'The Pouilly-Fuissé can bear to be kept in bottles for a long time; twenty years do not exhaust its strength and, on the contrary, adorn it with new graces.' Some 35 years after that was written, there must be few who keep any of their wines of the region that long.

Perhaps the peak of the wines of this appellation is found in the 'Vieilles Vignes' quality of the wine from Marcel Vincent of the Château de Fuissé. Because of the particular microclimate of the Château de Fuissé, the grapes ripen better than most of the Burgundian vineyards. The 1983 vintage was a particular case in point, when about a fifth of the grapes was affected by botrytis and extra yeasts had to be added to enable the wine to ferment out completely. The resultant wine is almost a freak, with more than 15 degrees of alcohol. It tastes full of fruit, warm, rich and seemingly lacking in balancing acidity, though apparently malo-lactic fermentation was prevented to minimise this failing. In a great vintage this is a fascinating construction of force and flavour. Another great wine is the Château de Beauregard, with about 20 hectares of vines in Fuissé. This label bears the words *tête de cru* which, whilst they suggest quality, have no official standing. Yet another good wine from Fuissé is the Clos du Bourg, from the domain of Roger Luquet. In a rather more delicate style are the wines of André Forest, whose vineyards are in the commune of Vergisson. The wines of Marc Bressand at Solutré have also given me much enjoyment.

It has been calculated that at least three-quarters of the total production of Pouilly-Fuissé is sold under the labels of the big merchant houses, so one can always select the wine from the company whose particular style you like. All the great names, the Bouchards, the Latours, the Drouhins will have their own Pouilly-Fuissé, but there is one small locally based company that specialises in the wines from the immediate locality of Pouilly-Fuissé. This is the house of Auvigue, Burrier, Revel, whose wines I have always enjoyed. For those interested in tasting on the spot, without committing themselves to visiting a grower, there is a tasting cellar and also an excellent hotel and restaurant, at Solutré.

It seems sad that one's tour round the white wine vineyards of Burgundy should finish on something of a low note, but if one starts in the north with Chablis, it seems only logical to finish in the south with the Beaujolais. The Beaujolais is a red wine region; it is here that the Gamay grape reigns supreme. Nevertheless some white Beaujolais is being made and though many of the vineyards that used to make white wine from the Chardonnay grape have now been transferred to the Saint-Véran appellation, I have the feeling that the figures for the production of white Beaujolais are increasing. It is interesting to note that plantings of the Chardonnay are being restricted to a maximum of a quarter of a property. This suggests that the authorities were beginning to think that some growers were too keen on cashing in on the white wine boom, whilst also profiting from the popularity of the name, Beaujolais. Another interesting development is that the producers of white Beaujolais are now numerous enough to have thought it worthwhile to create their own association to protect their interests. Despite all that I have said, the proportion of white wine in the Beaujolais is still no more than about 1 per cent of the whole.

To me white Beaujolais is a novelty, and, far too often, not a very interesting novelty at that. Most of the wines that I have tasted recently have been undistinguished. Nevertheless, there are certain wines upon which one can rely. Of the merchants, Louis Jadot, of Beaune, have regularly made something of a speciality of white Beaujolais under their own label. Of the single-vineyard names, it is perhaps Château de Loyse, at Romanèche-Thorins, which is the best known. The château, which dates back to the first half of the seventeenth century, and the vineyard belong to the Thorin family, at something over six hectares, is probably the largest single property producing white Beaujolais. The owners claim that the wine can rival the neighbouring cru of Pouilly-Fuissé. To me the wine is most enjoyable, but lacks some of the richness that one would expect from a Pouilly.

Two more recent discoveries for me are the Clos du Château de Lachassagne and the Château des Tours. The 1986 vintage of the former wine is perhaps the most enjoyable white Beaujolais that I have ever drunk, though it is fair to say that it was drunk under ideal circumstances; in brilliant sunshine at the La Terrasse des Beaujolais restaurant at Pommiers, which sits on the crest of a hill overlooking the vineyards. Certainly the wine had a fruit and flavour that is far too often lacking. The Château de Lachassagne belongs to Michel Gaidon, who also owns the Moulin à Vent vineyard of Château Porter, and who used to own Château de Pizay, which must be one of the most beautiful properties in the Beaujolais.

The vineyard of Château des Tours is perhaps best known for its wine of the Brouilly appellation. Of the 30 hectares of vines, something over one is planted in Chardonnay. These vines were planted some 15 years ago in such a way as to allow for machine harvesting, something which is still uncommon in much of the Beaujolais. The fermentation is temperature controlled, and over a period of ten days or so. The result is an average yield of some 6,000 bottles of a refreshingly crisp wine.

The wine road of Burgundy visits some strange places, but it is a popular route and attracts more pilgrims each year. Within the tight restrictions of a limited number of grape-varieties, methods of cultivation and vinification, there is a broad range of wines at widely varying prices; some high because of their intrinsic merits, others high because of their rarity value, sometimes even because of their novelty value. Great wines at fair prices can be found in Burgundy, but it is not often that they are found without a search. I hope that I have pointed out some of the signposts of this route which point to the more rewarding and enjoyable detours.

12
The Future
of White Burgundy

In the competitive wine world of today, what is the future for the white wines of Burgundy? This is a question that the wine trade has been asking itself for some years. Since the late 1960s, when the wines of Chablis and Pouilly-Fuissé first became known by a wider spectrum of consumers on the far side of the Atlantic, there has been recurrent pressure on producers to find enough wine to satisfy this demand. The answers have been many and varied. From my own experiences, I can recall one major shipper, not actually based in Burgundy, who stretched his Chablis with a judicious addition of white wine from Bordeaux. In another case a major American import house asked his supplier in Burgundy to ship him some Pouilly-Fumé as he felt that this customers would not recognise the difference from Pouilly-Fuissé, either in the way the label was spelt or in the quality of the wine.

Here, surely, is the root problem of the white wines of Burgundy. Most of them are bought by people who do not really know what they are drinking. They recognise one or two names, like Chablis or Pouilly-Fuissé, and are quite happy to plump for them when they see them on a wine-list. Whilst such vinous fundamentalism might well work with wines like Liebfraumilch and Mateus Rosé, where there are far fewer geographical constraints on the quantity of the wine produced, in quantitative terms Burgundy is a minute viticultural area. As has already been illustrated, the production of Burgundy, and especially white Burgundy, has increased dramatically over the last 25 years. At the same time, however, the number of wine drinkers with disposable income, and the interest, needed to drink such wines, has increased even more rapidly.

Apart from increasing production, the Burgundians have tended to deal with this increased demand in two different ways. Firstly, they have not hesitated to raise the prices. After all, white Burgundy is a commodity like oil and gold, and it is only plain economic sense to sell at the maximum price that you can expect for it. Or is it? The fact is that both oil and gold can be stored indefinitely without any deterioration in quality; white Burgundies have only a limited lifespan. In addition the demand for oil and gold is worldwide, whereas that for white Burgundy, in any appreciable quantities, is limited to comparatively few markets. Of these, potentially the most important, the United States, has shown itself to be very sensitive to currency fluctuations. When the French franc is weak against the dollar, the Americans buy, but when the dollar is weak, they seem to find their wines elsewhere.

The second move made by the merchants in Burgundy, more than anyone else, is to try to introduce the customer to some of those wines that he might not have met previously. Now every list includes white wines from villages such as Saint Romain, Auxey-Duresses and Rully, whereas, until recently such wines were offered more by the local growers. Indeed, if the appellation has not been there, in at least one case, the authorities have seen fit to create it. To follow on the skirt-tails of Pouilly-Fuissé, some of the vineyards that traditionally made Beaujolais blanc created the new name of Saint Véran. The broadening of the image of Burgundy, away from just a few names that were known to the majority of wine consumers, is a move in the right direction. First, it should help to maintain prices at reasonable levels, for it takes some of the pressure off the best-known wines. In addition, it must cut down the incentive for fraudulent labelling that has been only too common as far as some names are concerned. Many of the cases of wine-fraud that have been prosecuted in Britain over the past years have beeen because the customer has sought to buy wine, more often than not Chablis, at a price. There is always the dishonest supplier who is prepared to satisfy that demand.

Apart from the internal pressures on production, there are also those of competition from other sources. Whilst it might be said that the Pinot Noir produces its best wines in Burgundy and presents serious problems to the grower elsewhere, this is certainly not true of the Chardonnay. Just five years ago, California was considered to be the vineyard that might present the biggest challenge to Burgundy white wines. Now, this problem has receded to a great extent because importers in other countries have grown suspicious of currency rates and being trapped in a high-price source of supply. The second reason, and this is perhaps more fundamental, is that the growers of California's best wineries have realised that they can ask premium prices for their best wines. Thus, whilst the best wines of California might be as good as those from Burgundy, they are often more expensive.

The challenge to the Chardonnays of Burgundy is coming from a number of directions. Rapid advances in vinification techniques have meant that wines of good quality can now be offered not only from many parts of France, but also from around the world. Why has the Beaune company of Louis Latour planted extensively in the Ardèche? The answer can only be because they feel that they can make useful quantities of good wine there at better prices than they can in Burgundy. There are not the controls on the planting of new vineyards that there are in Burgundy, but the raw material is capable of producing wines that can honestly carry the prestigious name of Latour — and support the higher prices it demands.

Within France there are good Chardonnays being made in Haut-Poitou, the Jura and elsewhere. All of them are considerably cheaper than equivalent quality wines from Burgundy, yet their price is drawn up by the pressures on the white wines of Burgundy. Outside France there is also much competition from traditional wine-countries like Italy, and ones with a newer reputation, such as Bulgaria. Perhaps the most serious threat of all at the moment comes, however, from Australia and New Zealand. Both these countries have come late to the production of quality white wine, but they have learnt from the others. Both of them have comparatively weak currencies at the moment and, in Australia particularly, the cost of production is low due to the scale of the operations. This gives considerable economies both in the vineyard and in the cellars. Modern techniques can give high yields of quality wines. Perhaps they will very rarely attain the qualitative levels of the finest wines of, say, Puligny-Montrachet, but they often attain the levels of the plain village wines such as Rully or Auxey-Duresses at just a fraction of the cost.

Whilst the cost factor is not the only factor in Burgundy, it is an important one. It is illustrated by a piece by Louis Latour in his house journal.

Demand and shortage have fuelled each other to trigger huge price increases at the growers' level, none more dramatic than Pouilly-Fuissé, whose average price per barrel of 21 litres has risen from 4,000 francs for the 1982 vintage to 8,000 francs for the 1983 and 11,000 francs for the 1984. In dollar terms (at the exchange rates prevailing) the rises are not so spectacular: $602, $936 and $1160 respectively. Its fortunes are so closely linked to the dollar that recent falls on the currency market will help a return to stability, and will make it less difficult for our other markets to afford their share of the whites.

This was written in the autumn of 1985, but it illustrates well how susceptible the wines of Burgundy are to outside influences.

There is another, less obvious, message here. The vast increases in the prices of Pouilly-Fuissé bore no relationship at all to the intrinsic quality of the wine. It is probable that the wine of the 1984 vintage was of slightly lower quality than that of the 1982, and certainly lower than that of 1983. Nevertheless, there was this steady increase in price. Herein lies a major problem that few of the suppliers of the wine of Burgundy have appreciated. As market after market grows more sophisticated, so will there be a closer attention paid to the price that is offered for wine.

The fact is that there is far too much white Burgundy that is offered on the market that is of less than satisfactory standard. At a recent blind tasting of 61 white Burgundies, admittedly not in the highest price-bracket, but again not in the lowest, 28 I found to be of a quality that I would not enjoy drinking — and I do enjoy drinking, particularly white Burgundies. No less than eight of the wines were, in my opinion, out of condition and should not have been on the market. One can expect the occasional poor bottle of wine, but this proportion was unacceptable by anybody's standards. The criticism is not just aimed at the producers but also at the importers who submitted them for this tasting. Included in my rejection were wines from some of the most famous names in Burgundy, both merchants and growers. Whilst my feelings may not have coincided totally with those who were also tasting, they were representative of the general impression.

It is true that Burgundy must be on the fringes climatically for the making of fine wine, but this must demand more care on the part of the makers if they are to demand the prices they do. Even in the case of an excellent vintage like 1983, it is apparent that little thought went into the time when many growers picked their grapes or as to how they should deal with the exceptionally high sugar levels in the resultant musts. Perhaps such a vintage may only occur every 20 years, but any wine-student should know how to deal with it, and how to profit from it to make potentially exceptional wines.

The fact is that the Burgundian is very insular. For the most part he is prepared to say that the wines have been made this or that way for centuries and there is no reason to change. I can give two personal stories that illustrate this. One company whose wines I have criticised in the press on two occasions wrote to me complaining that they were a very successful company and that a writer in Canada said that they made the best of Burgundies. I replied that if they chose to accept his opinion, they had every right, but that I was also entitled to my own. However, I was quite happy to gain a further appreciation of their wines by tasting a range of wines selected by them, either in London or when I was next in

Burgundy. I have made such offers to two other companies and they have accepted the challenge. In this case it was ignored completely — even though it has since been repeated.

On another occasion, a very well-known winemaker from the other side of the world asked me if I could arrange for him to spend a vintage with a Burgundian company. The first one I approached was positively cool about the idea, on the rather contradictory grounds that they would have nothing to show such a renowned antipodean and that he would steal their ideas!

If the white wines of Burgundy are to maintain their pre-eminent role as the great dry white wines of the world, efforts will have to be made to tighten up on the control of the quality. All *appellation contrôlée* wines are now supposed to be submitting to tasting controls, before the *acquit vert* can be issued. Far too many wines seem to be below what one would expect the standard to be for the name on the label — and the price that is asked.

Whilst new techniques are being introduced in Burgundy, one feels that sometimes it is for the wrong reasons. One must welcome the introduction of more stainless steel into the cellars, but it should not be used to replace the oak cask for ageing purposes. As Robert Joseph pertinently points out in a recent article in *Wine Magazine*, 'What the Burgundians have to do is to concentrate on making the rich-yet-subtle wine that . . . other countries cannot easily manage. If the New World winemakers can afford to buy 300 bottle capacity new oak barrels at over £200 apiece from Burgundy (where else?) shouldn't the Burgundians be thinking of making a similar effort?' Traditionally the wines of Chablis were stored in small oak casks. Now there is only a handful of growers who use any oak at all. As a result Chablis has lost its personality and is too often just another Chardonnay in a host of competitors — yet at a price that is totally non-competitive. Even the use of other than new casks seems to be becoming rarer.

Appellation contrôlée in Burgundy was designed to keep the prices high by restricting the production. Now it has been liberalised in such a way as to allow greatly increased production at a time when the grower can get high prices. It is easy to be cynical about the whole quality factor in Burgundy. There are both growers and merchants who make continual efforts to offer fine white Burgundies, and some of them make rather better white wines than they do red, but there are too many who sell little more than the label on the bottle, because they have bought or made a wine with the documents that entitle them to do so. There is little finer than a great white Burgundy; there is little worse than a poor one.

Can Burgundy maintain its role and its image? I think that the answer is a qualified 'Yes'. The reason for this is peculiarly one of its weaknesses, the smallness of its size. Because of its rarity and its reputation, it will always remain in demand. There are new markets opening up all the time, and when one considers the current low levels of wine consumption in such supposedly sophisticated markets as the United States, Great Britain and Japan, one must be fearful as to whether the supply will ever approach the realistic demand. As disposable incomes become more important, so will wine-drinking increase. We should not forget that much of this generation is at least weaned on wine, even if it be in the comparatively humble form of coolers. If only the smallest fraction of that market moves on to the white wines of Burgundy in ten years time, then the pressure will be on.

There is of course the other reason that Burgundy can, and does, produce the finest of dry white wines. Whilst I am prepared to accept that Australia and California are capable of producing great Chardonnays, many of them in the Burgundy style, I have still to be convinced that at the very highest level they have yet made wines to match the very best from Burgundy. In wines, each consumer has his own idea of perfection; to me I have not tasted wines from outside Burgundy like the finest wines of Puligny and Meursault. I am sure that they can be made, and I am not saying that the best wines that are made are any worse, but there is still a place for the greatest Burgundies.

Perhaps there is one final reason. The white wines of Burgundy are part of a package. That package is Burgundy, its life and people, its food and its villages. Take away the white wines and something is missing. It may be an emotional reason to justify their continuing role, but I am convinced that it is a valid one.

I, personally, have a rather selfish outlook towards the whole problem. I want my wines to be available and I do not want to pay too much for them. Yet, at the same time, I want more people to share that pleasure with me. If there is to be a future for Burgundy and its white wines, it must come through those wines which are currently under-appreciated. The consumer will have to look to some of the lesser-known villages of the Côte and to the Hautes-Côtes, to the wines of the Côte Chalonnaise and the Mâconnais. But if we, as consumers, are to make this effort, and pay the price, to seek out these wines, we must demand a similar effort on the part of the producers. Bad wine must be eliminated and prices should equate to the innate quality of the wine. The grower cannot always control the latter, for there are often external financial pressures; however, the former is in his hands. It is his responsibility to marry what he can learn from new techniques to the centuries-old traditions of Burgundy. The end product though must be worthy of the reputation that has taken so long to create. May they remain as they were described by a Franciscan friar over 700 years ago, 'Fragrant, and comforting, and of excellent taste and they turn all who drink them to cheerfulness and merriment.'

Appendices

Appendix I: Vintages

How important is the vintage as far as the white wines of Burgundy are concerned? This is not an easy question to answer. As the vineyards lie on the theoretical frontiers of the geographical possibility for the making of good wines, weather is regularly an important factor. On the other hand, it is easier to make a reasonable white wine in a bad year than it is to make a good red. There are some who would say that the last truly disastrous vintage for white Burgundies was 1968, yet I have drunk many more than reasonable bottles from that year.

One other factor that must be taken into consideration is the potential life of the wine and when it will be at its peak. As I have said, the French tend to drink their white Burgundies much younger than the English. It is a matter of taste. As Pierre Poupon, one of Burgundy's more thoughtful drinkers, has written, 'Young wine, old wine . . . The first is comparable to virgin territory, lush, full of colour, wildness and life; the second to a spot full of history, humanity and wisdom, a place for meditation. You can enjoy them both, but you get different pleasure from each. To break into the first, you need the spirit of an explorer and, to land in the second, the mind of an archeologist.' These are the average times for maturing of the various white wines of Burgundy as given by the Comité National des Vins de France.

Mâcon blanc	1 to 3 years
Chablis	3 to 15 years
Pouilly-Fuissé	3 to 5 years (up to 8 years in exceptional vintages)
Meursault	5 to 20 years
Montrachet, Corton	8 to 20 years

In addition, I would add:

Bourgogne Aligoté	up to 3 years
Côte Chalonnaise	2 to 5 years
Lesser Côte d'Or	3 to 10 years
Puligny, Chassagne	5 to 15 years

With regard to the following notes on the vintages, I would stress that these must be taken as no more than guidelines. In Burgundy especially there always seem to be many exceptions, even to the most pragmatic of rules.

1987

This was one of those peculiarly Burgundian years when anything might have happened; the vintage could as easily have been a total disaster or a resounding success. In the end, as far as white wines were concerned, it finished up somewhere between the two.

A fine spring increased everybody's optimism for the wines of 1987, however cold and wet weather at the time of flowering led to a poor fruit set, with extensive *millerandage*. The summer weather was, for the most part, disappointing and there were few expectations. However, exceptional weather in September raised everybody's spirits again. At vintage time in October, the rain came again and the seesaw of morale continued. In the event, in Chablis and on the Côte d'Or, the opinion appears to be that the white wines lack the distinction of those of 1986. Whilst the better wines have plenty of finesse, there is not sufficient body to make them long-lasting.

As far as the Saône et Loire is concerned, there is more general satisfaction. Because of the lengthy spread of the flowering, those grapes that matured early made excellent wine, whilst more ordinary quality came from the more backwardly maturing regions. Nevertheless, generally speaking, the wines of Pouilly-Fuissé especially have good colour and are round, soft and full-bodied. Throughout Burgundy, the quantity of wine made was less than the average of the previous years, but with the collapse of the American market, particularly for white Burgundies, this did not cause any particular concern.

For most of the wines of the region, the consumer would be wiser to select his white wines from the 1986 vintage rather than the 1987, though, as with every year, there are exceptions to the rule.

1986

The general comment about this vintage amongst the growers seems to be, 'If 1986 had not followed 1985, it would have been considered to have been a great vintage.' Due to an extremely cold and long winter, the vines were slow to develop. However excellent weather from the middle of June until the middle of August gave promise of good wine. Rain during the latter half of August and much of September caused spirits to fall, but a fine end to the month and beginning of October meant that those who had not rushed into picking in the rain, made some very good wine.

Louis Latour in his vintage report calls 1986 'A Chardonnay Year' and graphically describes the benefit of the late sunshine, 'The amazing story is that this sudden upturn was felt from North to South, from Chablis to Mâcon, for a crop nearly equal in size to 1982. The Grands Crus harvested late, like the Corton-Charlemagne, will easily reach 13.5 and even 14 degrees of sugar. The best Pulignys and Meursaults were at 12.5/13 and the wisdom of the Mâcon growers paid handsomely: starting on the 3rd of October, they immediately climbed the scale of quality with wines which will be equal if not better than many of the 1985s.

'The Chablis area, which appeared to be doomed to mediocrity by the late picking date and the huge size of the crop, was suddenly producing wines which could be among the best of the past decade.'

Throughout Burgundy very good white wines were made with a fine balance of fruit and acidity. Prices fell sharply, particularly in Chablis and the Mâconnais, so this is a vintage that represents good value for money.

1985

Someone said of this vintage in Burgundy that it was impossible to make bad wine. The vintage took place in ideal conditions after a hot August and September. One problem would appear to be a lack of acidity in many wines from the Mâconnais, which now appear rather dull and lifeless. On the other hand, those growers who took care made excellent wines. In Chablis, many outstanding wines were made, as also on the Côte d'Or and the Côte Chalonnaise.

1984

Sandwiched between two 'vintages of the century', the reputation of the white wines of 1984 has tended to suffer. This is a pity, for I have much admired their lean elegance, which comes as a pleasant contrast to the blowsy opulence of many of the wines of both 1983 and 1985.

1983

A very hot summer with little rainfall, followed by a wet September and perfect vintage time meant rather unbalanced wines. Perhaps the vintage succeeded best in Chablis, where fine balanced wines were made. Elsewhere, lack of acidity has caused many wines to fall apart quickly and this is a year when the winemaker had to take extra care. Generally speaking this is a vintage with an overblown reputation, deserved only by a minority of the wines that were made. In addition the wines were expensive, so one runs the risk of having some costly disappointments.

1982

This harvest produced the highest yield on record and the result is that the individual characteristics of many wines have been diluted. The growers who picked early, with sufficient acidity in the grapes, made wines which are still showing well. The others will now probably be over the top. It is worthwhile seeking out the best bottles as they should be at reasonable prices.

1981

A year which shows that one cannot generalise about the wines of Burgundy. There were heavy frosts in Chablis, which led to a severely reduced crop there. During the summer there was a shortage of sun and during the crucial months of June and September the rainfall was exceptionally heavy. Nevertheless, throughout Burgundy, elegant white wines were made, though the crop was generally low. This is the classic example of the point that it is easier to make white wines in what is considered to be a bad vintage, for the reputation of the red wines is not high.

1980
This was a late harvest of wines that started with an excess of acidity. For the best wines, this has enabled them to hold together and they can still show well. However, lesser wines have now fallen apart and should be avoided.

1979
A large vintage, which nevertheless gave excellent white wines. Apart from the best wines from the Côte d'Or, these will now probably be past their peak.

1978
A small yield of top-quality wines, with very concentrated flavours. This is a year when the finest wines will last well and be outstanding examples of white wines which will keep and, in some cases, improve.

1977
The whites of this year were better than the reds, but both have now passed into blessed oblivion.

1976
Wines that were high in alcohol, but low in acidity. As a result most have now maderised.

1975
A wet year which produced a few great wines on the Côte d'Or. In Chablis, on the other hand, the summer was fine and dry, so excellent wines were made and one can still find the occasional *grand cru* wine of real class.

1974

Spring frosts caused considerable damage in Puligny, Chassagne and Meursault and heavy rain in September spoilt what might have been great wines. One would be unlikely to find any white wine of interest from this year now.

1973

A big vintage of agreeable, elegant wines that have turned out to be better adapted to the sprint than the long-distance event.

1972

Wines of this year had very high initial acidity, which meant that only the greatest showed well, and some of these are still most agreeable, though they are hard to find.

1971

A small vintage of excellent, concentrated wines. The only likely survivors are *grands crus* from the Côte d'Or and an occasional Chablis.

1970

Soft, easy wines that will now have faded away.

1969

A first-class vintage of wines that were for some time rather backward. These have now developed and most have begun to decline. Nevertheless, the best wines from the Côte d'Or should still show well.

1968

Now of only historical interest, and not very pleasant history at that.

Older vintages where it might be possible to find an occasional bottle of white Burgundy of interest: 1966, 1964, 1961, 1955, 1953.

Appendix II: White Wine Appellations of Burgundy

	Area	Average Production Years 1975–84	Best Vineyards
YONNE			
Chablis Grand Cru	100.12 has	5300 hls	see page 57
Chablis Premier Cru	610.26	30350	see page 57
Chablis	1240.14	58900	
Petit Chablis	134.46	6000	
Sauvignon de Saint Bris	54	4000	
CÔTE D'OR			
CÔTE DE NUITS			
Fixin		9 (1984 vintage only)	
Morey-Saint-Denis		34	Monts Luisants
le Musigny		8	
Vougeot		45	Clos Blanc
Nuits Saint Georges		17	La Perrière, Clos Arlots
Côte de Nuits-Villages		21 (but 157 hls in 1984)	
CÔTE DE BEAUNE			
Ladoix-Serrigny		127	
Aloxe-Corton		19	
Corton		49	
Corton-Charlemagne	71.88	1245	
Charlemagne	62.94	No declaration of crop	
Pernand-Vergelesses		542	
Savigny-les-Beaune		329	
Chorey-les-Beaune		13	
Beaune		463	Clos de Mouches, Clos Saint Landry
Côte de Beaune		153	
Monthelie		64	
Auxey-Duresses		1079	

159

	Area	Average Production Years 1975–84	Best Vineyards
Saint-Romain		1089	Sous Roches, Combe Bazin
Saint-Aubin		960	En Gamay, les Murgers, La Chatenière, les Dents de Chien
Meursault		13723	Les Gras (3.55has), les Charmes (47.96), les Perrières (14.65), les Genevrières (16.48), les Porusots (11.43), les Bouchères (4.41), les Gouttes d'Or (5.32), la Jeunelotte (5.04), Sous Blagny (2.21), La Pièce sous le Bois (11.15), Sous le Dos d'Ane (5.03)
Puligny-Montrachet		8657	les Chalumeaux (5.79), Champ Canet (4.06), la Garenne (11.4), Sous le Puits (6.8), Hameau de Blagny (4.28), la Truffière (2.48), Champ Gain (10.7), les Folatières (17.64), Cailleret (3.93)
le Montrachet	7.998	266	
Chevalier-Montrachet	7.36	183	
Bâtard-Montrachet	11.87	451	
Bienvenues-Bâtard-Montrachet	3.69	144	
Chassagne-Montrachet		5221	see page 93
Criots-Bâtard-Montrachet	1.57	54	
Santenay		180	les Gravières
Dezize-les-Maranges		22 (1984 vintage only)	
Sampigny-les-Maranges		No declaration of crop	
Cheilly-les-Maranges		7 (1983 vintage only)	
SÂONE ET LOIRE *CÔTE CHALONNAISE*			
Rully		3200	
Mercurey		1050	
Givry		500	
Montagny	426.41	3800	
Bourgogne Aligoté Bouzeron		950	
MÂCONNAIS			
Mâcon		1100	
Mâcon Superieur		8200	
Mâcon-Villages		95000	

	Area	Average Production Years 1975–84	Best Vineyards
Saint-Véran		15800	see page 134
Pouilly-Loché		1200	
Pouilly-Vinzelles	120	2000	
Pouilly-Fuissé		15800	see page 139
RHÔNE			
Beaujolais		2000	
GENERIC			
Bourgogne Grand Ordinaire		2400	
Bourgogne Aligoté		45500	
Bourgogne		9500	
Bourgogne Hautes-Côtes de Nuits		800	
Bourgogne Hautes-Côtes de Beaune		400	

Appendix III: Recommended Producers

This list is of those names that have been recommended in the main body of the text for each appellation. After are given the relevant addresses of the wine makers or distributors in alphabetical order. It must be pointed out that this by no means includes all the producers of fine white Burgundies, but is based solely upon my own experiences. Another point worth noting is that most of the names that are given are of growers, whilst probably two-thirds or more of all Burgundy that is sold appears under the label of a merchant. Many of these merchants are mentioned in the text, where they actually have vineyards or a speciality, but, almost of necessity, they do not receive the attention in the text that they might deserve. Most of the major merchants of Beaune and Nuits Saint Georges carry a range of white wines from throughout Burgundy. Among such merchants whose white wines I particularly like are Joseph Drouhin, Louis Jadot, Prosper Maufoux (who also often appears under the name of Marcel Amance) and Louis Latour. On a more regional basis, I would nominate Henri Laroche, Régnard, Moreau and Lamblin in Chablis, André Delorme on the Côte Chalonnaise and Georges Duboeuf, Loron and Mommessin in the Mâconnais.

BOURGOGNE GRAND
ORDINAIRE

Cave des Vignerons de
Buxy, Buxy
Roland Viré, Chitry

BOURGOGNE ALIGOTÉ

Ch. de Davenay, Buxy
Dubreuil-Fontaine, Pernand-
Vergelesses
Lamblin et Fils, Maligny

BOURGOGNE ALIGOTÉ
BOUZERON

Bouchard Père et Fils,
Beaune
Chanzy Frères, Bouzeron
A. et P. de Villaine,
Bouzeron

BOURGOGNE BLANC

Clos de la Chaînette,
Auxerre
Chanson Père et Fils, Beaune
Louis Latour, Beaune
Ets. Leroy, Auxey Duresses
Ch. de Meursault,
Meursault

CHABLIS

Bacheroy-Josselin, Chablis
La Chablisienne, Chablis
René Dauvissat, Chablis
Droin Père et Fils, Chablis
Jean Durup (Domaine de
l'Eglantière), Maligny
William Fevre (Domaine de
la Maladière), Chablis
Alain Geoffrey, Beines
Lamblin et Fils, Chablis
Henri Laroche, Chablis
A. Long-Depaquit, Chablis
J. Moreau et Fils, Chablis
Société Civile de la
Moutonne
A. Régnard et Fils (Albert
Pic), Chablis
Simonnet-Fèbvre et Fils,
Chablis
Robert Vocoret, Chablis

MEURSAULT

Robert Ampeau et Fils,
Meursault
J.-F. Coche-Dury, Meursault
Jean Germain, Meursault
Hospices de Beaune, Beaune
Patrick Javillier, Meursault
Domaine des Comtes Lafon,
Meursault
René Manuel, Meursault
Joseph et Pierre Matrot,
Meursault
G. Michelot, Meursault
Ropiteau Frères, Meursault
Domaine Ropiteau-Mignon,
Meursault
Societe d'Élevage et de
Conditionnement de Vins
Fins, Meursault

BLAGNY

Ch. de Blagny, Blagny
Henri Clerc et Fils, Puligny
Montrachet

PULIGNY–MONTRACHET

Robert Ampeau et Fils,
Meursault
Jean Chartron, Puligny-
Montrachet
Chartron et Trébuchet,
Puligny-Montrachet
Henri Clerc et Fils, Puligny-
Montrachet
Joseph Drouhin, Beaune
Domaine Laroche, Puligny-
Montrachet

Domain Leflaive, Puligny-Montrachet

Domaine Étienne Sauzet, Puligny-Montrachet

LE MONTRACHET

Bouchard Père et Fils, Beaune

Marquis de Laguiche, Chassagne-Montrachet

Domaine Leflaive, Puligny-Montrachet

Domaine Jacques Prieur, Meursault

Domaine de la Romanée-Conti, Vosne-Romanée

Baron Thénard, Givry

CHEVALIER—MONTRACHET

Bouchard Père et Fils, Beaune

Jean Chartron, Puligny-Montrachet

Henri Clerc et Fils, Puligny-Montrachet

Louis Jadot, Beaune

Louis Latour, Beaune

BÂTARD—MONTRACHET

Henri Clerc et Fils, Puligny-Montrachet

Delagrange-Bachelet, Chassagne-Montrachet

Joseph Drouhin, Beaune

Albert Morey et Fils, Chassagne-Montrachet

Ramonet-Prudhon, Chassagne-Montrachet

Domaine de la Romanée-Conti

BIEN VENUES—BÂTARD—MONTRACHET

Louis Carillon et Fils, Puligny-Montrachet

Henri Clerc et Fils, Puligny-Montrachet

Domaine Leflaive, Puligny-Montrachet

Ramonet-Prudhon, Chassagne-Montrachet

Domaine Étienne Sauzet, Puligny-Montrachet

CRIOTS—BÂTARD—MONTRACHET

Delagrange-Bachelet, Chassagne-Montrachet

CHASSAGNE—MONTRACHET

Jean-Marc Blain-Gagnard, Chassagne-Montrachet

Delagrange-Bachelet, Chassagne-Montrachet

Jean-Noel Gagnard, Chassagne-Montrachet

Marquis de Laguiche, Chassagne-Montrachet

Duc de Magenta, Chassagne-Montrachet

Albert Morey et Fils, Chassagne-Montrachet

MARSANNAY

Domaine Fougeray de Beauclair, Marsannay

FIXIN

Bruno Clair, Chassagne-
Montrachet

MOREY SAINT DENIS

Domaine Ponsot, Morey-
Saint-Denis

VOUGEOT

L'Heritier-Guyot, Vougeot

MUSIGNY

Domaine Comte Georges de
Vogüé, Chambolle-
Musigny

NUITS SAINT GEORGES

Jules Belin, Premeaux
Domaine Henri Gouges,
Nuits Saint Georges

CORTON BLANC

Hospices de Beaune, Beaune
Domaine Chandon de
Briailles, Savigny
Daniel Sénard, Aloxe-
Corton

CORTON CHARLEMAGNE

Domaine Bonneau de
Martray, Pernand-
Vergelesses
Bouchard Père et Fils,
Beaune
Domaine Maurice Chapuis,
Aloxe-Corton

Dubreuil-Fontaine, Pernand-
Vergelesses
Hospices de Beaune, Beaune
Domaine des Héritiers
d'Hyppolite Thévenot,
Savigny
Louis Jadot, Beaune
Louis Latour, Beaune

ALOXE–CORTON

Daniel Sénard, Aloxe-
Corton

PERNAND–VERGELESSES

Chanson Père et Fils,
Beaune
Jacques Germain, Chorey-
les-Beaune
Domaine Laleure-Piot,
Pernand-Vergelesses

SAVIGNY

Capron-Manieux, Savigny
Jean Chénu et Fils, Savigny

BEAUNE

Bouchard Père et Fils,
Beaune
Joseph Drouhin, Beaune

CÔTE DE BEAUNE

Maurice Joliette, Beaune

AUXEY–DURESSES

Robert Ampeau et Fils,
Meursault

André Guillemard-Pothier,
Meloisey
Ets. Leroy, Auxey-Duresses
Duc de Magenta,
Chassagne-Montrachet
Michel Prunier, Auxey-
Duresses

SAINT—ROMAIN

Fernand Bazenet, Saint-
Romain
Ropiteau Frères, Meursault
Roland Thévenin, Santenay
Rene Thévenin-Monthélie et
Fils, Saint-Romain

SAINT—AUBIN

Maison Raoul Clerget,
Saint-Aubin
Domaine Jean Lamy et ses
Fils, Saint-Aubin

SANTENAY

Maison Prosper Maufoux,
Santenay

HAUTES CÔTES DE NUITS ET DE BEAUNE

Cave Cooperative des
Hautes-Côtes, Beaune
Ets. Geisweiler, Nuits Saint
Georges
Domaine Guillemard-
Dupont, Meloisey
Bernard Hudelot, Villars-
Fontaine
Domaine Thévenot le Brun
et Fils, Marey les Fussey

MERCUREY

Bouchard Ainé et Fils,
Beaune
Maison J. Faiveley, Nuits
Saint Georges
Domaine Michel Juillot,
Mercurey
Antonin Rodet, Mercurey

RULLY

André Delorme, Rully
Domaine de la Folie,
Chagny
Ets. Meulien-Pigneret, Rully
Pierre-Marie Ninot, Rully
Domaine de la Renarde,
Rully
Ch. de Rully, Rully
Domaine Saint-Michel,
Santenay

GIVRY

André Delorme, Rully
Maurice Derain, Moroges
Jean-Pierre Ragot, Givry
Remoissenet Père et Fils,
Beaune
Baron Thénard, Givry

MONTAGNY

Cave des Vignerons de
Buxy, Buxy
Ch. de Davenay, Buxy
Louis Latour, Beaune
Ch. de la Saule, Montagny

MÂCON/MÂCON–VILLAGES

Domaine de la Bon Gran,
Clesse
Cave Cooperative de
Chaintré, Chaintré
Cave Cooperative de Clessé,
Clessé
Cave Cooperative d'Igé, Igé
Cave Cooperative de Lugny,
Lugny
Cave Cooperative de Prissé,
Prissé
Cave Cooperative de Viré,
Viré
Jacques Dépagneux,
Villefranche sur Saône
Joseph Drouhin, Beaune
Louis Latour, Beaune
Ets. Mommessin, Mâcon
Piat Père et Fils, La
Chapelle de Guinchay
Domaine du Prieuré, Lugny
Domaine de Roally, Viré
Domaine Talmard, Uchizy
Domaine Thévenet, Clessé
Domaine Thévenet-Wicart,
Clessé

SAINT VÉRAN

Cave Cooperative de Prissé,
Prissé
Chanut Frères, Romanêche-
Thorins
Georges Duboeuf,
Romanêche-Thorins
Domaine R. Duperron,
Leynes

Henri-Lucius Gregoire,
Davayé
Lycée Agricole de Davayé,
Davayé
Ets. Mommessin, Mâcon
Marcel Vincent, Fuissé

POUILLY–LOCHE/POUILLY-VINZELLES

Cave des Grands Crus
Blancs, Vinzelles
Georges Duboeuf,
Romanêche-Thorins
Loron et Fils, Pontanevaux
Jean Mathias, Chaintré
Ch. de Vinzelles, Vinzelles

POUILLY–FUISSÉ

Auvigue, Burrier, Revel,
Charnay-les-Mâcon
Ch. de Beauregard, Fuissé
Clos du Bourg, Fuissé
Marc Bressand, Solutré
André Forest, Vergisson
Ch. de Fuissé, Fuissé
Roger Luquet, Fuissé
Marcel Vincent, Fuissé

BEAUJOLAIS BLANC

Louis Jadot, Beaune
Clos du Château de
Lachassagne, Lachassagne
Ch. de Loyse, Romanêche-
Thorins
Ch. des Tours, St Etienne-
la-Varenne

Appendix IV: Suppliers' Addresses

Robert Ampeau et Fils, 6, rue du Cromin, 21190 Meursault

Auvigue, Burrier, Revel, Le Moulin du Pont, Charnay-les-Mâcon, 71000 Mâcon

Fernand Bazenet, Saint-Romain, 21190 Meursault

Château de Beauregard, 71960 Fuissé

Jules Belin, S.A.R.L., Prémeaux-Prissey, 21700 Nuits Saint Georges

Jean-Marc Blain-Garnard, route de Santenay, Chassagne-Montrachet, 21190 Meursault

Domaine de la Bon Gran, *see* Domaine Thévenet

Domaine Bonneau de Martray, Pernand-Vergelesses, 21420 Savigny-les-Beaune

Bouchard Ainé et Fils, 36, rue Ste Marguerite, 21200 Beaune

Bouchard Père et Fils, au Château, 21200 Beaune

Clos du Bourg, *see* Luquet

Marc Bressand, le Bourg, 71960 Solutré-Pouilly

Nicole et Jean Marie Capron-Manieux, rue de Bourgogne, 21420 Savigny

Louis Carillon et Fils, Puligny-Montrachet, 21190 Meursault

Cave Cooperative de Chaintré, 71570 Chaintré

Cave Cooperative de Chardonnay, 71700 Chardonnay

Cave Cooperative de Clessé, 71260 Clessé

Cave Cooperative des Hautes-Côtes, route de Pommard, 21200 Beaune

Cave Cooperative de Lugny, 71260 Lugny

Cave Cooperative de Prissé, 71960 Prissé

Cave Cooperative de Viré, 71260 Viré
Cave des Vignerons de Buxy, 71390 Buxy
Cave des Grands Crus Blancs, 71145 Vinzelles
La Chablisienne, 89800 Chablis
Ch. de Chamirey, distributed by Antonin Rodet q.v.
Domaine Chandon de Briailles, 21420 Savigny
Chanson Père et Fils, 10, rue Paul Chanson, 21200 Beaune
Chanut Frères, Route du Moulin à Vent, 71570
    Romanèche-Thorins
Chanzy Frères, Domaine de l'Hermitage, Bouzeron, 71150
    Chagny
Clos du Chapitre, distributed by Jacques Depagneux q.v.
Domaine Maurice Chapuis, 21420 Aloxe-Corton
Domaine Jean Chartron, Grande Rue, Puligny-Montrachet,
    21190 Meursault
Ets. Chartron et Trebuchet, Puligny-Montrachet, 21190
    Meursault
Ch. de Châtelard, distributed by Bouchard Ainé et Fils q.v.
Ets. F. Chauvenet, 6, rue de Chaux, 21700 Nuits Saint
    Georges
Jean Chénu et Fils, les Mollots, 21420 Savigny
Bruno Clair, Chassagne-Montrachet, 21190 Meursault
Henri Clerc et Fils, Puligny-Montrachet, 21190 Meursault
Maison Raoul Clerget, Saint-Aubin, 21190 Meursault
J.-F. Coche-Dury, 21190 Meursault

René Dauvissat, 8, rue Emile Zola, 89800 Chablis
Ch. de Davenay, distributed by Picard Père et Fils, q.v.
Domaine Delagrange-Bachelet, Chassagne-Montrachet,
    21190 Meursault
André Delorme, Domaine de la Renarde, Rully, 71150
    Chagny
Jacques Dépagneux, 21, rue du College, 69400 Villefranche
    sur Saône
Maurice Derain, 71390 Moroges
Domaine des Dîmes, distributed by Chanut Frères q.v.
Droin Père et Fils, 3, rue de Montmain, 89800 Chablis
Joseph Drouhin, rue d'Enfer, 21200 Beaune
Ets. Georges Duboeuf, 71570 Romanèche-Thorins

Domaine P. Dubreuil-Fontaine Père et Fils, Pernand-
Vergelesses, 21420 Savigny
R. Duperron, 71570 Leynes
Jean Durup, Domaine de l'Eglantière, 89800 Chablis

Domaine de l'Eglantière, *see* Jean Durup
Domaine de l'Évêque, distributed by Ets. Mommessin q.v.

Maison J. Faiveley, B.P. 9, 21700 Nuits Saint Georges
William Fèvre, Domaine de la Maladière, 14, rue Jules-
Rathier, 89800 Chablis
Domaine de la Folie, Fully, 71150 Chagny
André Forest, le Bourg, 71960 Vergisson
Domaine Fougeray de Beauclair, 21160 Marsanay-la-Côte
Ch. de Fuissé, *see* Marcel Vincent

Jean-Noel Gagnard-Dupont, Chassagne-Montrachet, 21190
Meursault
Maison Geisweiler et Fils, 2, rue de la Berchère, 21700
Nuits Saint Georges
Alain Geoffroy, 4, rue de l'Equerre, Beine, 89800 Chablis
Domaine Jacques Germain, au Château, Chorey-les-
Beaune, 21200 Beaune
Jean Germain, 9, rue de la Barre, 21190 Meursault
Domaine Henri Gouges, 7, rue du Moulin, 21700 Nuits
Saint Georges
Henri-Lucius Grégoire, 71960 Davayé
Guillemard-Dupont Frères, Meloisey, 21190 Meursault
André Guillemard-Pothier, Meloisey, 21190 Meursault

L'Héritier Guyot S.A., 21640 Vougeot
Domaine des Héritiers Hyppolite-Thévenot, 21420 Aloxe-
Corton
Domaine des Hospices de Beaune, 21200 Beaune
Bernard Hudelot, Villars-Fontaine, 21700 Nuits Saint
Georges
Patrick Javillier, 7, Impasses des Acacias, 21190 Meursault
Maurice Joliette, la Montagne, 21200 Beaune
Michel Juillot, 71640 Mercurey

Domaine des Comtes Lafon, Close de la Barre, 21190
Meursault
Domaine Laleure-Pilot, Pernand-Vergelesses, 21420
Savigny
Lamblin et Fils, Maligny, 89800 Chablis
Jean Lamy et ses Fils, St Aubin, 21190 Meursault
Domaine Laroche, 10 rue Auxerroise, 89800 Chablis and
au Château, Puligny-Montrachet, 21190 Meursault
Maison Louis Latour, 18, rue des Tonneliers, 21200
Beaune
Domaine Leflaive, Puligny-Montrachet, 21190 Beaune
Ets. Leroy, Auxey-Duresses, 21190 Meursault
A. Long-Depaquit, 45, rue Auxerroise, 89800 Chablis
Ets. Loron et Fils, Pontanevaux, 71570 La Chapelle de
Guinchay
Ch. de Loyse, distributed by Thorin q.v.
Roger Luquet, 71960 Fuissé
Lycée Agricole de Davayé, 71960 Davayé

Domaine du Duc de Magenta, Abbaye de Morgeot,
Chassagne-Montrachet, 21190 Meursault
Domaine de la Maladière is distributed by William Fèvre
q.v.
René Manuel, 21190 Meursault
G.A.E.C. Mathias, 71570 Chaintré
Domaine Pierre et Joseph Matrot, 21190 Meursault
Maison Prosper Maufoux, Place du Jet d'Eau, 21590
Santenay
Ets. Meulien-Pigneret, *see* André Delorme
S.C. Domaine du Château de Meursault, au Château,
21190 Meursault
Domaine G. Michelot, 31, rue de la Velle, 21190
Meursault
Ets. Mommessin, La Grange Saint Pierre, B.P. 504, 71008
Mâcon
J. Moreau et Fils, Route d'Auxerre, 89800 Chablis
Albert Morey, Chassagne-Montrachet, 21980 Meursault
G.F.A. La Moutonne, 89800 Chablis

171

Pierre-Marie Ninot, Rully, 71150 Chagny

Piat Père et Fils, 71570 La Chapelle de Guinchay
Albert Pic, *see* A. Régnard
Picard Père et Fils, Route de Saint Loup de la Salle, 71150
  Chagny
Domaine Ponsot, Morey-Saint-Denis, 21200 Gevrey-
  Chambertin
Domaine Jacques Prieur, 2, rue des Santenots, 21190
  Meursault
Domaine du Prieuré, 71260 Lugny

Jean-Pierre Ragot, rue de la Planchette, 71640 Givry
Domaine André Ramonet-Prudhon, Chassagne-Montrachet,
  21190 Meursault
Rapet Père et Fils, Pernand-Vergelesses, 21420 Savigny
François Raveneau, 9, rue de Chichée, 89800 Chablis
A. Régnard et Fils, 28, bvd Tacussel, 89800 Chablis
Remoissenet Père et Fils, 20, rue Eugène Spuller, 21200
  Beaune
Domaine de la Renarde, *see* André Delorme
Domaine de Roally, 71260 Viré
S.C. de la Romanée-Conti, Vosne-Romanée, 21700 Nuits
  Saint Georges
Ropiteau Frères, 21190 Meursault
S.C. Domaine Ropiteau-Mignon, 11, rue du 11 Novembre,
  21190 Meursault
Château de Rully, Comtes d'Aviau de Ternay, au Château,
  Rully, 71150 Chagny

Domaine Saint-Michel, 21590 Santenay
Château de la Saule, Alain Roy-Thévenin, 71390
  Montagny-les-Buxy
Domaine Étienne Sauzet, Puligny-Montrachet, 21190
  Meursault
Domaine Daniel Sénard, 21420 Aloxe-Corton
Simonnet-Fèbvre et Fils, 9, ave Oberwesel, 89800 Chablis
Societe d'Élevage et de Conditionnement de Vins Fins,
  21190 Meursault

Paul et Philibert Talmard, 71700 Uchizy
Philippe Testut, Ch de Grenouille, 89800 Chablis
Domaine Thénard, 7, rue l'Hotel de Ville, 71640 Givry
Domaine Jean Thévenet, rue Quintaine, 71260 Clessé
Thévenet-Wicart, *see* Domaine Jean Thévenet
Roland Thévenin, Haut de Santenay, 21590 Santenay
Domaine Rene Thévenin-Monthélie et Fils, Saint-Romain,
    21190 Meursault
S.A.R.L. Thévenot-le-Brun et Fils, Marey-les-Fussey, 21700
    Nuits Saint Georges
Ets. Thorin, 71370 Romanèche-Thorins
Ch. des Tours, Domaine des Tours S.C.I., St Etienne la
    Varenne, 69830 St Georges de Reneins

A. et P. de Villaine, Bouzeron, Bouzeron, 71150 Chagny
Marcel Vincent, au Château, 71960 Fuissé
Mme. Roland Viré, 89530 Chitry-le-Fort
Robert Vocoret et Ses Fils, 16, rue Émile Zola, 89800
    Chablis
Domaine Comte de Vogüé, 21220 Chambolle-Musigny

Bibliography

ANDRIEU, Pierre: *Petite Histoire de la Bourgogne et de son Vignoble*, Montpellier, La Journée Vinicole, n.d.

ARLOTT, John and FIELDEN, Christopher: *Burgundy Vines and Wines*, Revised Edition, London, Quartet Books, 1978.

ARNOUX, Mr: *Dissertation sur la Situation de Bourgogne*, London, Samuel Jallasson, 1728.

(BAVARD, Abbé E.): *Notice sur le Vignoble et le Vin de Volnay*, Dijon, J.-E. Rabuton 1870.

BAZIN, Jean-François: *Le Vignoble des Hautes-Côtes de Nuits et de Beaune*, Les Cahiers de Vergy, n.d.

—— *et al*: *Le Vin de Bourgogne*, Lausanne, Editions Montalba, 1976.

BÉGUILLET: *Nouveau Traité de la Vigne avec la Meilleure Méthode de la Cultiver*, Dijon, Edmé Bidault and Toulouse, Dupleix et Laporte, 1773.

BENOIT, Felix and CLOS-JOUVE, Henry: *La Bourgogne Insolite et Gourmande*, Paris, Solar, 1975.

BLANCHET, Suzanne: *Les Vins de Bourgogne*, Marmande, Editions Jéma, 1985.

BRÉJOUX, Pierre: *Les Vins de Bourgogne*, Paris, L. Larmat, 1967.

BUSBY, James: *Journal of a Tour through some of the Vineyards of Spain and France*, Sydney, Stephens and Stokes, 1833.

CANNARD, Henri: *Balades en Bourgogne, Guide des*

Vignobles de Chablis et de l'Auxerrois, Dijon, Henri Cannard, 1983.

——: *Balades en Bourgogne, Guide des Vignobles de la Côte d'Or*, Dijon, Pornon, 1984.

——: *Puligny Montrachet et son Vignoble*, Dijon, author, 1988.

CHAPUIS, Louis: *Vigneron en Bourgogne*, Paris, Robert Laffont, 1980.

CHIDGEY, Graham: *Guide to the Wines of Burgundy*, London, Pitman, 1977.

CLOS-JOUVE, Henry: *Le Promeneur Lettré et Gastronome en Bourgogne de Dijon à Lyon*, Paris, Amiot Dumont, 1951.

—— and BENOIT, Felix: *Le Beaujolais Secret et Gourmand*, Paris, Solar, 1973.

(COURTEPÉE): *Histoire Abrégée du Duché de Bourgogne*, Dijon, Causse, 1777.

DANGUY, R. and AUBERTIN, Ch.: *Les Grands Vins de Bourgogne*, Dijon, Armand, 1892.

Les Délices de la Campagne, Paris, Pierre Des-Hayes, 1654.

DÉLISSEY, J. and PERRIAUX, L.: *Les Courtiers Gourmets de la Ville de Beaune*, Dijon, Centre d'Études Bourguignonnes, n.d.

DENMAN, James L.: *The Vine and its Fruit*, 2nd Edition, London, Longmans, Green and Co., 1875.

Détails Historiques et Statistiques sur le Département de la Côte d'Or, Dijon, Gaulard-Marin, 1818.

DOUTRELANT, Pierre-Marie: *Les Bons Vins et les Autres*, Paris, Seuil, 1976.

DROUOT, H. and CALMETTE, J.: *Histoire de Bourgogne*, Paris, Boivin et Cie, 1928.

DUIJKER, Hubrecht: *The Great Wines of Burgundy*, London, Mitchell Beazley, 1983.

DUMAY, Raymond: *la Mort du Vin*, Paris, Stock, 1976.

EISENCHTETER, M: *Bévy: The Birth of a Burgundy*, Nuits Saint Georges, Bourgogne Geisweiler, n.d.

——: *Le Bourgogne au 18ème Siecle*, Nuits Saint Georges, Bourgogne Geisweiler, 1983.

——: *Choosing Burgundy*, Nuits Saint Georges, Bourgogne Geisweiler, n.d.

FOILLARD, Leon and DAVID, Tony: *Le Pays et le Vin Beaujolais*, Villefranche en Beaujolais, Jean Guillermet, 1929.

FONDET, Maurice: *Le Domaine et les Vins de l'Hôpital de Beaune*, Beaune, René Bertrand, 1910.

FORGEOT, Pierre: *Origines du Vignoble Bourguignon*, Paris, Presses Universitaires de France, 1972.

——: *Pélerinage aux Sources du Bourgogne*, Colmar, S.A.E.P., 1971.

GENRET-PERROTTE: *Rapport sur la Culture de la Vigne et la Vinification dans la Côte d'Or*, Dijon, Loireau-Feuchot, 1854.

GEORGE, Rosemary: *The Wines of Chablis*, London, Sotheby, 1984.

GINESTET, Bernard: *Chablis*, Paris, Jacques Legrand-Nathan, 1986.

GREGORY OF TOURS: *History of the Franks*, trans. Lewis Thorpe, London, Penguin Books, 1974.

GRIVOT, Françoise: *Le Commerce des Vins de Bourgogne*, Paris, Sabri, 1964.

GUILLAUME, André: *La Côte d'Or*, 2nd Edition, Dijon, 1963.

(GUILLEMOT): *Pétition Concernant le Ban de Vendange*, Dijon, Simonnot-Carion, 1835.

GUNN, Peter: *Burgundy: Landscape with Pictures*, London, Victor Gollancz, 1976.

GUYOT, Dr Jules: *Sur la Viticulture du Centre Nord de la France*, Paris, Imprimerie Impériale, 1866.

GWYNN, Stephen: *Burgundy*, London, Constable, 1934.

HANSON, Anthony: *Burgundy*, London, Faber and Faber, 1982.

HATCH, Evelyn M.: *Burgundy Past and Present*, London, Methuen, 1927.

JOHNSON, Hugh: *Wine Companion*, London, Mitchell Beazley, 1983.
——: *The World Atlas of Wine*, 3rd Edition, London, Mitchell Beazley, 1985.
JULLIEN, A.: *Topographie de Tous les Vignobles Connus*, 2nd Edition, Paris, Madame Huzard, 1822.

LANDRIEU-LUSSIGNY, Marie-Hélène: *Le Vignoble Bourguignon, ses Lieux-dits*, Marseille, Jeanne Laffitte, 1983.
LARMAT, Louis: *les Vins de Bourgogne*, Paris, Larmat, 1952.
LAURENT, Robert: *Les Vignerons de la Côte d'Or au XIXe Siècle*, Paris, Société des Belles Lettres, 1958.
LAVALLE, Dr J.: *Histoire et Statistique de la Vigne et des Grands Vins de la Côte d'Or*, Paris, Dusacq, 1855.
LICHINE, Alexis: *Wines of France*, 3rd edn, London, Cassell, 1956.
LUCHET, Auguste: *La Côte d'Or à Vol d'Oiseau*, Paris, Michel Lévy Frères, 1858.

MALTE-BRUN, V.-A.: *Côte d'Or*, Dijon, 1882.
MARIE, Annick: *Le Grand Livre de la Cuisine Bourguignonne*, Paris, Jean-Pierre Delarge, 1977.
MARION, Maurice: *Illustration et Défense du Vin de Beaune*, Beaune, Syndicat de Défense des Interêts Viticoles de Beaune, n.d.
MARTIN, Germain: *Essai sur la Vente des Vins (Plus Particulièrement des Vins de Bourgogne)*, Dijon, Barbier-Marilier, 1904.
MATHEY, Adalbert: *Mercurey et ses Vins*, Bordeaux, Imprimerie Bordelaise, 1883.
MILLER, Philip: *The Gardeners Dictionary*, 2nd edn, London, C. Rivington, 1733.
de MOUCHERON, E.: *Grands Crus de Bourgogne*, Beaune, Dupin, 1955.

Nouvelle Maison Rustique, Paris, Desaint, 1772.

des OMBIAUX, Maurice: *Nouveau Manuel de l'Amateur de Bourgogne*, Paris, L. Rouart and J. Watelin, 1921.

ORDISH, George: *The Great Wine Blight*, London, J.M. Dent, 1972.

PÉRRIAUX, Lucien: *Histoire de Beaune et du Pays Beaunois*, Paris, Presses Universitaires de France, 1974.

PIC, Albert: *Le Vignoble de Chablis*, Paris, 1935.

PITIOT, Sylvain and POUPON, Pierre: *Atlas des Grands Vignobles de Bourgogne*, Paris, Jacques Legrand, 1985.

(PLAIGNE): *L'Art de Faire, d'Améliorer et de Conserver les Vins*, Turin, les Frères Reycends, 1783.

Plan Statistique des Vignobles Produisant les Grands Vins de Bourgogne, Beaune, Batault-Morot, 1861.

POMEROL, Charles (ed.): *Terroirs et Vins de France*, Total, Paris 1984.

POUPON, Pierre: *Nouvelles Pensées d'un Dégustateur*, Bibliothèque de la Confrérie des Chevaliers du Tastevin, Nuits Saint Georges, 1975.

——: and FORGEOT, Pierre: *A Book of Burgundy*, London, Lund Humphries, 1958.

——: *Les Vins de Bourgogne*, 1st ed and subsequent ones in French and English, Paris, Presses Universitaires de France, 1952.

PUVIS, M.-A.: *De la Culture de la Vigne et de la Fabrication du Vin*, Paris, Dusacq, 1848.

REDDING, Cyrus: *A History and Description of Modern Wines*, London, Whittaker, Treacher and Arnot, 1833.

ROBINSON, Jancis: *The Great Wine Book*, London, Sidgwick and Jackson, 1982.

——: *Vines, Grapes and Wines*, London, Mitchell Beazley, 1986.

RODIER, Camille: *Le Clos de Vougeot*, Dijon, L. Vienot, 1949.

——: *Le Vin de Bourgogne*, Dijon, L. Damidot, n.d.

ROUGET, Charles: *Les Vignobles du Jura et de la Franche-Comté*, Lyon, Auguste Côte, 1897.

SAINTSBURY, George: *Notes on a Cellar-Book*, London, Macmillan, 1920.

SEWARD, Desmond: *Monks and Wine*, London, Mitchell Beazley, 1979.

SUTCLIFFE, Serena: *The Wines of Burgundy*, London, Mitchell Beazley, 1986.

—— (ed.): *Great Vineyards and Winemakers*, London, Macdonald, 1981.

THEURIET, Charles: *Histoire de Nuits Sous-Beaune*, 1886.

THUDICHUM, J. L. W.: *A Treatise on Wines*, London, George Bell and Sons, 1896.

VANDYKE PRICE, Pamela: *French Vintage*, London, Harrap, 1986.

VERGNETTE-LAMOTTE, M. de: *Mémoires sur la Viticulture et l'Oenologie de la Côte d'Or*, Dijon, Douillier, 1846.

VERMOREL, V. and DANGUY, R.: *Les Vins du Beaujolais, du Mâconnais et Chalonnais*, Dijon, Armand, n.d.

VINCENOT Famille: *Cuisine de Bourgogne*, Paris, Denoël, 1979.

YOXALL, H. W.: *The Wines of Burgundy*, 2nd edn, London, Pitman, 1978.

Articles in *Decanter, Wine, The Wine Spectator, Wine and Spirit, Bourgogne, Tastevin en Main, The House Journal, L'Art Culinaire*.

Index